THE UNBROKEN THREAD

E. Ruth Harder

A Russian Hill Press Book
United States • United Kingdom • Australia

Russian Hill Press

Cover and Book Designer: Coleen Royal
Library of Congress Control Number: 2019918181
ISBN: 978-1-7341220-2-2

Dedication

I would like to dedicate The Unbroken Thread in memory of my parents, Alvin and Elsie Dornbusch, who instructed me in basic life skills, and gave me a firm foundation on which to build my life.

Acknowledgements

Many people helped me in the creation and publication of The Unbroken Thread.

I am grateful to all who encouraged me to write: my children, grandchildren, sisters and friends, the Holy Cross Lutheran church family in Livermore California, the Faith Lutheran Church family in Kamiah, Idaho.

California Writers Club, Tri-Valley Writers have given me valuable information and support. George Cramer secured beta readers Sally Kimball, Gary Lea, and Lani Longshore who handled my manuscript with great care and insight. I am very grateful to them as I could not have done it as well without their input.

I'm indebted to Paula Chinick of Russian Hill Press who kept me on task.

Violet Moore, line editor, did a thorough reading, comments and correction of the manuscript. Her knowledge of Biblical history and faith are invaluable to me.

Coleen Royal, who created my fabulous cover design as well as the book's interior design, is not only a talented artist, but also my daughter.

To God be the glory, because without his guidance I could not have created the character Meydl Tabitha and this work of Biblical historical fiction.

THE UNBROKEN THREAD

One

My plan was to stay away until my family came searching. I kept running, past the crooked grapevines and toward a rocky, dusty trail I found. Since I had not ventured beyond the area where I could see our house, the bushy terrain was all new to me. I did not know where I was going and did not care. My legs grew weary, so I sat in the shade of a tree no taller than me. I am almost a woman, too old to cry, yet I gave in to great face-wetting tears I wiped with my sleeve. Why did Father not want to let me change my name from Meydl to Tabitha? I thought he did not love me as much as he did my sisters Naomi and Phoebe. If my family did not look for me, it must mean I was right. He did not love me. I looked at a grasshopper on a twig and wondered if his life was as bad as mine.

I thought it would be great if it were to rain and soak me now. Perhaps I would become sick and die. Would they be sorry? No clouds appeared, and I snuffled into my hands. The sun was warm, and I drowsed.

I awakened when a shadow loomed over me. I did not look up at first, supposing it was my mother. "Hello, meydl," a young man said. I saw a boy, about my age, standing wide-legged, barefoot, toeing the earth. My life-blood drummed.

"How did you know my name?"

"I do not know it and called you meydl," he squeaked, then cleared his throat.

"Sadly, it is also the name I was given."

"No one has that name, so you must be a servant's child," he sneered, deepened his voice, "but you are not dressed like a slave. Tell me who you really are."

"I will not tell you more." I remained seated, weak-kneed. "Why do you want to know?"

"Because you do not belong here. You are on my property, and I will force you off if you do not leave." He made a fist but kept it at his side.

"I am beside the trail where all people travel. It can be no crime to rest on my journey."

"Where are you going?" He was dressed in the plain tunic and short striped cloak of a local farmer.

"You are asking questions, so I will ask one. What is your name?"

"What if I do not want to tell you?" He lifted his pointed chin when he said it.

"How old are you?" I tried to sound like Mother when she questioned us girls.

"What difference does it make?" His lip curled.

"You are older than me, yet you cannot be old enough to own property. Now let me be," I said and stood, a head shorter than he. "I have forgotten something at home and need to go back before I can continue my trek." I gave his arm a push to shove him out of my way. "Be gone."

Startled at first, he lifted an arm as though he would knock me down but lowered it as I kept moving. "It has been a pleasure, beautiful meydl," he sneered.

Openmouthed, I stopped walking and turned around to squint at him.

He made an ugly face at me and waggled his tongue. "I will marry you someday."

My face grew hot. "Would you marry a slave?" I had not spoken with any boy before, knew nothing about the ways of men, and certainly did not want to continue this conversation.

"You will be mine and do as I ask." His voice became gruff and mean.

I turned and ran toward my home, at least I hoped I was going in the right direction. My life pulse pounded in my chest. He ran faster and sped past, then blocked my path, so I ran into him. He grabbed my arms and tried to force them behind my back. "Stop. Stop it," I spat out at him. During the struggle, I tripped over a root and stumbled.

"Make me." He bent over me, and his tongue waggled and licked my pursed lips. "Do you like this? I have more."

"No, go away," I said, trying to rise, gasping for breath. Helpless and humiliated,

I was afraid and wanted to go home.

"I have more to show you. You will enjoy it so much you will not want me to stop."

Desperate tears wanted to surface, but I could not let him see how weak I felt. Words would not come, and he clamped his hand over my mouth so I could not scream. He straightened his body suddenly, let go, and shoved me. I fell and rolled in the dry scratchy grass and dust, ready to run if I could make my legs move. I turned as I stood, saw him saunter away, and he ran when he thought I no longer watched. I heard faint voices calling in the distance.

I walked on the trail toward our vineyard and then to the well where I dipped the bucket and drew water to wash the grime from my face where the boy had put his tongue on me. The air was still and suffocating. Nobody called me, so I supposed the cries I had heard were for him. I started toward the house and stopped when I saw Mother approach. Even if she scolded, I was happy to see her.

With the danger of attack now gone, the drumming in my chest slowed some, but I was shaken like never before. Earlier, my sisters had taunted me, and what happened afterward was the reason I had foolishly wanted to go far from home. As I waited for Mother, what they had said was fresh in my mind.

My sister Naomi began in a lilt, and Phoebe joined

in. "Meydl, Meydl get us some water to drink. Why are you walking so slowly? We will beat you if you do not hurry." Their dark curls bobbed up and down as their words spewed out. They did not hit me, but their teasing left me in tears. I could do nothing about their mean treatment, but I had no one else to play with. I hated my name because it simply meant "girl." Sometimes I seethed with anger, and I wanted to run to places unknown. Often, I walked around in our small vineyard and enjoyed the grass or sand squishing under my feet.

The start of the day had been beautiful, and the anemones bloomed red in the meadows where we lived some distance from Jerusalem. My father's large olive grove extended far to the right of our house, and next to it were grapevines growing in the field by the well. The barley pasture was to the other side. My plain beige tunic flapped about my calves in the breeze as I watched the grassy field where the goats grazed. I never tired of looking at the way the wind moved the grass so it shone lighter in the sunlight, then shifted to darker green. While I was tempted to linger, my thoughts turned to my mother who surely could use a helping hand with the many tasks required to care for our home and family. Being with her took my mind off the sadness I was feeling.

She had been bent over the dry barley on the stone where she was pulverizing seeds to make flour. Her dark, curly hair tied in a thin strip of leather hung to her waist. "Mother, may I help with grinding meal?"

"Thank you, no, I would like for you to take the soiled dishes." Mother stopped speaking. When she saw my tear-stained face, she asked, "What ails you, Meydl?"

"I wish I had a real name, not Meydl." I snuffled tears, feeling ashamed I had complained.

"Why do you want to change your name?" When I was silent, she said, "I have heard the teasing, but it is harmless." She set the mortar aside on the stone, opened her arms and embraced me. I was thirteen, but I clung to her as I had not been hugged for a long time. It felt good to have her smooth my light brown wavy hair from my brow. She stopped to look at me. "What name would you like?"

"Any name—not Meydl." I felt shy about having mentioned it, but I could not take back what I had asked. I desperately wanted a new name. Perhaps I could pray to the Lord in heaven far away, but I doubted he would hear an insignificant girl like me.

Last week, I helped Mother light the candles for Purim, a celebration honoring Queen Esther. Her bravery in speaking with her husband, King Ahasuerus, saved her fellow Jews from destruction. We are a people who worship the Lord whose name we cannot say. I believe in YHWH as all my ancestors have and thought about how the Lord had used a woman to help his people. I continued my kitchen chores as these thoughts occupied my mind.

I gathered the soiled bowls and utensils and put them into a large bucket of water to soak. I wiped my tears with my sleeve and tried to think of a name I would like. We worked quietly as my sisters chattered outside. It felt good to be inside doing woman's work. Mother was kind, and I did not feel like a girl slave people did not call by a real name.

"Would you like the name Tabitha? Mother dumped the flour she had ground into a stone jar for storage.

"*Talitha.* That name is no better." I sulked.

"The name I said was Tabitha." Mother pronounced it, putting emphasis on the first part, and it sounded nice.

"Tabitha. I like that name." I was lighthearted. As I stacked the clean dishes on the shelf, I thought how wonderful it was to be Tabitha.

"I have mending to do. Would you like to learn to sew?" Mother gathered some items in a basket.

"Yes, I would." I decided it had to be more fun than doing dishes.

We sat on a straw mat in the shade of the house. She drew out a needle. "It is made from bone. See the eye in the needle, a hole where you must insert this thread before you begin." She gave it to me.

I picked up the end of the thread and tried several times to poke it through the tiny hole. The thread spread out in a little fringe at the end so it was impossible to put it there. "I cannot do it," I sighed.

"Here, I will show you." She wet her forefinger with a bit of saliva and rubbed the thread between her wet finger and her thumb. She put the tamed end into the eye of the needle and pulled through the length of light brown thread. "I would like for you to mend this seam in your tunic, so space your stitches evenly."

"Thank you." I was grateful the needle was threaded. It was a worn garment I had not seen recently because it had been in Mother's mending basket. When I looked at the tear, I gained some confidence. "It is a few stitches." She watched as I poked the needle in and out of the cloth as she instructed. I kept sewing and finished the seam.

Mother smiled. "I see you will not need much practice."

"I have watched you many times and thought how wonderful it would be to make things." It seemed natural to have a needle in my hand as I mended the tunic easily.

"Here are two pieces of plain fabric I cut out to make a simple tunic. Sew the seams to put the two parts together." She laid them one atop the other. She poked the needle into the seam and back out with even stitches. "Now you try it. Keep the two pieces held fast by your left hand and be sure you catch both. Do not pull the thread tightly."

I was eager to do as she had done. She watched. "Good, Meydl. Now, tie a knot as you did for the mended seam so the thread is secured."

I became overconfident, plied the threaded needle into the material, and drew it tight quickly. The thread snapped as I pulled in haste. Perplexed, I knew the broken thread needed a knot. I tied it. "Have we not an unbreakable thread?"

"No, I have not seen it." She stood, smiled, patted my arm.

I became immediately distracted. "I see Father going to the well for water. Can we meet him there and ask him to bless me as Tabitha?" Mother smiled and nodded. We set our sewing aside and hurried out.

"Stephen, I want to talk with you." Mother came to the well and gave him a dipper of water.

"Thank you, Erna. What news makes your face glow beautifully? Are we to have a son?" He smiled at her.

"No, I have another matter." Mother shook her head, smiled up at him. "Meydl is becoming of age, and you will be finding a husband for her. She needs a real name." Mother's face was serene and gentle.

"What is wrong with what I named her?" He pursed his lips and folded his arms across his ample chest.

"Nothing, I suppose, but I thought it was time to give her a different one." She bent her head at first, and I feared she would say no more. But she straightened, stood as tall as she could, and her voice was strong as she said, "Tabitha."

The name hung in the air unanswered. The breeze stopped, I held my breath and I felt heat rising to my head. I wanted to run and hide but thought better of it. I cowered behind my small mother and watched Father's expression change. It was as if a shadow had fallen on him.

He scowled and said, "I am used to calling this daughter Meydl. Meydl, come here," he commanded.

I slipped from behind my mother to stand obediently in front of him and hear him announce my new name. I bowed my head, waited for his blessing. "Yes, Father?" My heart quickened in anticipation, as I longed to feel his hand on my head.

"See, she answers to Meydl." He had patted me on the head. "I have work to do." He gulped the last of the water from the dipper, turned, and strode toward his fields.

My devastation and disappointment had been almost unbearable. I wanted to hate him. I wondered how my parents would ever find a husband for me, a mere meydl. Would people think I was a servant? I had never wanted to see my father or sisters again. But after the trauma of attack by the boy on the trail, I was very relieved to see Mother.

"Did you have a nice walk?" As she came near, the worry lines softened from her brow. She stopped suddenly and reached out to me. "Did you fall? Your garments are dirty and your face is reddened." She hugged me to her.

"Yes, but I'm all right now." I decided not to tell her about the encounter with the nasty boy because it would upset her to hear of it.

"Your father did not mean to make you unhappy."

"Oh, why does he not want me to have a proper name?" I grabbed Mother's hand.

"Sit here in the shade," she said as we came to an olive tree. The air was cooler and felt fresh.

"I will try to explain something we should have told you but always felt could wait." She sat facing me.

"What is it, Mother? You look sad." My face grew hot as I looked at her, wondered what she was about to say about who I really was. My life pulse drummed.

She paused, wiped her hands on her tunic, and her voice shook as she said, "I am not your birth mother."

Two

I felt prickly all over and wondered if I was born of a slave as the boy had suggested. It seemed as if the sun stood still in its course across the heavens. "Mother, please let me know," I pleaded.

"My hands were the first to hold you," she said. "I was the midwife and could save you, but not your mother."

"No," I wailed. She reached out to me and we embraced. Her body was shaking, weeping with me.

She looked into my eyes. "Your father was in such anguish and disbelief, he could not think clearly enough to give you a proper name. He called you meydl, and I thought it was temporary, but he has never changed his mind."

"Tabitha was my birth mother's name?"

She nodded. "I nursed you and my baby Naomi who was eight months old. I knew much sorrow because my husband died before he knew I was with child."

"You married my father." I began to fill in the story.

"Yes. When the year's mourning time had passed, we wed." She stood and dusted her clothing.

"You are my mother, the only mother I have known." As I rose and we embraced, her warmth and love comforted me. "Now I understand why Father does not want to name me Tabitha. Do I look like her?"

"Yes, you are beautiful with hazel eyes and lighter wavy hair like your mother's. When I look at you, I think of her, and I am sure he does too. It is why I thought he might want you to have her name."

"Thank you for telling me." I felt troubled and although I wanted to run and leap like a gazelle, I trudged slowly toward the vineyard where I could sit among the gnarled grapevines. Mother went to the house, and sensing I wanted time to think, did not ask me to come.

I sat down again to take in all I had learned about my birth and was at peace. The warm breeze lifted my hair and I felt caressed. I heard footsteps and thought it might be Naomi or Phoebe, but they were heavier. It was Father, his voice awash with relief. "There you are." He swiped one hand against another as I had seen him do endless times when a matter had been finished.

"I am sorry, Father. I did not know . . ."

"And your mother has told you?" His brow softened, and his shoulders relaxed as he crouched down next to me.

"Yes, she told me about my birth, and my mother's

name was Tabitha. I would like you to tell me more about her."

He looked off across the fields toward the mountains in the far distance. He sighed and sat beside me. "We were together forever, or so it seemed. Our parents knew each other and visited often. It was natural for my father to make a promise with Tabitha's father so she would become my wife. We were young and delighted we could be with each other again as we had played together when we were children. Her name was the same as a beautiful, graceful gazelle, and she ran like one. She and I raced and jumped high in the air, seeing who could leap over the tallest grass. When I reached the age of bar mitzvah, we no longer were allowed to be alone together until our betrothal. We loved each other, and with our parents' blessings, we married." He stood, hesitated, and his eyes told me how much he cared for me.

I reached for my father's hands, and he helped me up. While hurt he had not told me the circumstances of my birth before, I felt honored he took time to be with me and tell me a little about my mother. He gathered me in his arms and held me for a long time, something I could not remember him doing. Neither of us spoke for a time.

"Thank you," I whispered. He let go of me and looked away. I knew he had tears on his face he did not want me to see. He turned and left me standing among the vines. My head ached, yet I felt satisfied inside.

I walked toward the house and fondled the young smooth vine branches and rough older grapevines. I decided they were all the same yet different, as my sisters and I were. I mused over how to make peace with them, as they were the only friends I had. I tried to think of things they would like to do instead of my own interests. They saw me coming.

Phoebe met me, grabbed at my arm and ran to get a comb. "Please braid my hair." She plopped down in front of me, her curls a thick dark brown nest waiting to be tamed. Before now, I would not have tried unless Mother asked me to do it. "I want my hair to look like yours."

When she looked at me, I saw admiration in her eyes and decided to be playful. "What will I do with this?" I dug the comb into the center of her crown and waited, pretending it was hopelessly stuck in tangles. "You have given me an impossible task." I tugged again.

"Stop it," she squealed and reached up to slap my free hand.

When I giggled, she joined in and Naomi laughed. We kept up the mock tragedy of Phoebe's hair, although I could apply water to tame, comb and braid it. Naomi sat and braided her own. Although she and I were almost the same age, I thought I was too old to play with her and Phoebe. I wanted to do something interesting with my time.

Mother watched us, amused. "A young woman lives nearby who recently married our neighbor Samuel. His farm is the one by neighbor Asa's. Her name is Lottie, and I will invite her to come meet you."

I was elated to make a friend of a young woman near my age and hoped she would be a nice person. At last, she came up the trail to visit with us. When she stopped at the door to remove her sandals, I sat and washed her feet. She giggled when I touched her foot, and I knew instantly we would be friends. "My feet are sensitive," she said. Her face reddened, yet she seemed self-assured.

"Mine are too, Lottie. I am Meydl, and this is Naomi and Phoebe. Come sit where we can talk." Her soft round lips formed an arc and her cheeks dimpled as her dark eyes sparkled with joy.

"Thank you. I hope we can be good company. When I married, I moved away from my family to be with Samuel and his olive groves. My parents are more than two days walk from here." Lottie smoothed her tunic with plump hands as she settled her roundish body on the floor cushion. "I am happy to have new friends."

"I am glad you came. Would you like wine?" I offered her a cup and set out a plate of flatbread and goat cheese.

"I will enjoy it," she said.

Mother and my sisters sat as we supped and carried on light conversation.

"Who does the needlework I see on top of the basket there?"

"It is my stitching. Mother has taught me and I

enjoy it." I tried not to sound proud.

"I have done small repairs on my garments, but nothing more. Sewing is a good skill to learn." Lottie nodded her head.

I liked Lottie.

She came bustling up as I sat sewing. "My husband Samuel is always busy at work in the fields, and I hardly see him. I am glad to be here with you."

"I am sewing again."

"I will love to watch while we talk."

Naomi and Phoebe sat nearby and giggled. Naomi's dark eyes gleamed as she brought her sewing and sat with us.

Lottie settled beside me and we talked amiably. It made me happy to have a friend. I stitched. I had not yanked on the thread, but it broke.

"I am sixteen. How old are you?" Lottie's eyes were upturned and expressive as she spoke.

"Thirteen, fourteen later this year," I said. I tied the thread and again wondered if there was such a thing as a stronger one.

"I am fourteen and Phoebe is eleven." Dark-haired Naomi stood as tall as she could, a little more than Phoebe.

"Have your parents selected husbands for you?" Lottie's broad brow was creased, and she wiped a stray hair off her cheek and tucked it behind her ear.

Naomi shook her head. Phoebe said, "I hope they wait until I am old enough because I do not want to be alone."

"They have not told me about a husband. I think of myself as common because of my name, Meydl."

"Yes, you are no longer little Meydl." Lottie tossed her long black braid from side to side and smiled. "Our neighbor Asa is showing Samuel how he handles the barley planting. "Did you know Asa has two eligible sons? Jacob is the eldest and diligently works with his father. His younger brother is lazy. He often goes into the town and drinks with his friends. You and Naomi could marry them."

"Naomi is older than me so she would get the hard-working man. The other one would be left for me," I said. Naomi and Phoebe giggled.

Three

Almost a year had passed. As I sat outdoors sewing, an inner joy and contentment flowed from my head to my hands. The air was pleasantly cool, and I heard the boisterous sounds of men calling to one another in the barley field where they were working. I stitched in even strokes with my needle as I embroidered a silken curled-leaf design on a linen scarf. My mind drifted to what life would be as a grown woman, perhaps with children tugging at my skirt. I smiled, thinking of my friend Lottie, when Father's voice interrupted my daydream.

"Meydl," Father called from inside the house.

Startled, I jabbed my finger with a needle. "Yes, Father." My thread severed, and I put my bleeding finger in my mouth.

"Come," said Mother, her voice excited. "We have something to tell you."

I hurried and wondered what they had to say.

Perhaps Father decided I could be named Tabitha. I felt hopeful and joyful. The two of them sat on the bench where they usually supped. Mother patted the place next to her, and I sat.

"We have spoken with neighbor Asa. He has two sons," Father said.

"We have decided . . ." Mother began. Father lifted a hand gently and placed it on her shoulder.

"The eldest is the most responsible and will inherit the land when his father dies." Father's expression was calm and unexpressive as if he were handling business.

I waited and looked at him, and then to Mother, disappointed this was not about my name.

"I believe he will be the most suitable husband for you." Father rubbed his graying chin whiskers and looked at my face.

"I think you will like him," Mother said.

"Thank you." I was surprised, confused beyond words. Naomi was not mentioned, and she was a little older than me.

"He is willing to pay the bride's price for you, and his father agrees. Asa has been ill and wants to see his sons settled in marriage soon," Father said.

"We will need the year to prepare and to make you a lovely wedding garment." Mother's eyes shone with excitement.

"Do you have anything you wish to say, Meydl?" Father glanced at me, not expecting any disagreement.

"Is he old?" I spoke without thinking. Surprised,

but not excited, I did not want to say anything to make Father angry. I knew he cared because he had taken time out of his day to speak with me about this important matter.

"I believe he is thirty-five or so. He looked at Mother, who nodded. "He owns barley fields and olive groves. His father has cattle, sheep, and goats. We are fortunate to live in this fertile valley. I trust he will provide bountifully."

I stared at the clean brown earthen floor and tried to think of something to say in response, but no words would form. I looked up at Mother who was smiling graciously. I glanced at Father, whose face had the satisfied appearance of having sold his grain for a good price. Quietness consumed the air like a lull before a downpour.

Father nodded, braced himself with his hands on his knees as he stood. "It is settled. I must go attend to my fields. If you need anything, you know where I may be found."

I felt as if I had fallen and had no breath. What would it be like to leave my family and live with a man and his family? I did not peer up at Mother as I went outside to clear my head.

"Meydl, Meydl!" Naomi met me as I came out. "What do you think? Did they find a nice husband for you? Who is it? Tell us all about him. I am the oldest, and you cannot be the first to marry." Naomi's eyes squinted with envy.

"They made us stay outside while you talked." Phoebe pouted. "But we could hear a little. When will you be going away?"

"One question at a time." I smiled at their sisterly eagerness. "It will at least be a year, Phoebe. I think it will be well with me, and yes, they found a good husband who is a property owner and an older man."

"Old? Will you be feeding him broth in bed and wiping drool from his mouth?" Naomi raised an eyebrow. Phoebe giggled.

"Perhaps." I frowned to play along with the idea. "Naomi, I think you should have this old man since you are my elder. Since I am younger I must ask your forgiveness if I marry him."

"I want a husband, but not an old one," she wailed. "I forgive you. You can have him."

I laughed, grabbed my sisters in an embrace. "No, silly, he is not so old. He is a strong, handsome man, and he works hard in his fields." I hoped I was right. "He has a brother, Naomi."

We were joyful together, and I thought how good it was to have sisters who no longer made fun of my name. Mother let us all share in lighting the candles for our Sabbath meal. Father said the prayers. I could see how important it was to keep the rituals of our faith, and I intended to keep our Sabbath practices when I had my own home. It took forever for the day to come when I would meet my future husband. At last, we were on our way there.

My feet gathered dust as I scuffed along in my new sandals. My parents were dressed well: Father, in the soft brown cloak he wore to the synagogue, and Mother in a long green tunic and sash. We spoke little on our walk in the brisk air. Anticipation of this day had my mind going in all directions, like a shifting wind, between feelings of joy and dread, nervousness and laughter. I wanted the day to happen and yet looked forward to it being over.

We were at the neighbor's door in front of a home a little larger than ours. Asa hobbled up behind his servant, who had opened the door. "Please, please come in." A small dark woman, smiling graciously, stood behind Asa as we all walked in. "Thank you," he said, dismissing his servant.

"Stephen, Erna, this my son Uzziah, and this is Menat, my wife."

Uzziah had a startled expression on his face, and my face burned red. I was ready to run in another direction. While the slender boy had matured some since our encounter on the trail about a year ago, I knew I would not like him to be my husband. He greeted my parents, grinned briefly at me, murmured something inaudible, and left the room. I wondered if he was the man I was to marry, as I had not been given a name.

"Please come this way," Asa led us to another room. "Here is Jacob, your intended bridegroom." He gestured toward his handsome son.

"And our Meydl Tabitha," Father said. He beamed, grasped my elbow and urged me to step beside him.

My mouth was open in awe and relief, and I breathed deeply to compose myself. Tabitha! Father had added Tabitha to my name. Jacob was a half head taller than my father with broad shoulders and wore a fine brown vestment and a leather girdle about his middle. His sandals laced high on his muscular calves. What impressed me was his air of ease and authority. My parents had indeed made a good choice.

I thought about how my appearance might be to his eyes. Mother had braided my hair and then released the ends of the plaits to create shiny tresses showing beneath a yellow cotton scarf. I wore a new, pale yellow linen tunic with my embroidered sash. A gift of new leather sandals from my parents was the envy of my sisters. I was confident, yet anxious, as the conversation began.

The meal went well. Uzziah did not return, as Jacob and I were the center of attention of our parents. Asa excused himself to go into another room a couple of times when we were supping and talking. Jacob shook his head and said, "His ailment seems worse." Menat nodded.

Asa came in and cleared his throat. "Stephen, the wedding will take place one year from today unless some need arises to move the date." He kissed my father on both cheeks, and father returned the formality.

"Have we agreed on the wedding price?" Jacob

summoned a servant to come with the wine, poured my father another goblet of fine red liquid, and offered more to Mother, Menat, and me.

"Yes, I am pleased with Jacob's offer of seven goats, one homer of barley, and ten flasks of olive oil." Father had a relaxed pleasant look about him. My palms were wet with sweat, but I felt altogether excited and satisfied with the day.

"I would be remiss if I did not tell you how joyful I am." Jacob raised his glass in my direction, smiled broadly, and asked my father, "Shall we agree to meet in a week when my future lovely bride and I can go through our formal engagement?"

Father stood and lifted his cup. "It is agreeable, *L'Hayim!*"

"To health and life! Welcome to our family, Meydl Tabitha. May the year pass swiftly." Jacob's father nodded.

"Thank you," I said. All I could think about was Jacob had called me lovely, so he was as pleased with my appearance as I was with his.

"I am sorry for the dreaded cough making our visit short, or I would arrange the *erusin* today." Jacob's father clasped arms with my parents. The servant saw us out.

Outside the front door, I was surprised to see Uzziah sitting in the shade drinking from a pewter cup. He lifted his other hand and waved to us but gazed at me, winked, and a broad smile creased his cheeks. I looked away.

Our families met the following week for the erusin, our official engagement.

Lottie and Samuel were invited to be our witnesses. When she and I saw each other, we kissed cheeks warmly. She was overjoyed for me.

Samuel and Lottie offered three prayers. After each prayer, Jacob took a sip of wine and handed the pewter cup to me to take a sip. "To health, to life!" echoed in the room. My hand shook as I took the wine cup.

The warmth of strong red wine filled my mouth and slowly seeped into my body. A deep sense of fulfillment of my womanhood imbued me with thoughts of the wonderful married life I envisioned.

On our way home, I asked Mother if I could make a cloak as a gift for Jacob. She said, "A cloak would be a sweet gift from your own hands."

Mother brought me two choices of cloth from a shopping trip to Jerusalem, one brown and one undyed gray wool. I chose light brown, sturdy lamb's wool fabric. When I first began sewing, I was excited and pulled abruptly on the thread. It severed. Dissatisfied I had to slow down, I longed for unbreakable thread. I tried to be more careful sewing. Day after day, I made straight stitches, but they were not perfect and there were times I picked out an entire seam to resew.

I learned to be patient. Hours also went into preparation for the wedding. Mother was sewing my wedding garments. It was an exciting time and some days the hours flew fast, on others the moments felt like hours. At last, I admired the finished cloak, imagined how handsome Jacob would look in it, and hoped he would like it.

Four

O n our wedding day as agreed, father accepted the gifts of goats, barley, and flasks of olive oil from Jacob. Besides our families, many neighbors attended. The wedding guests walked in a processional line until they came to my father's house where I waited. Dressed in finery—layers of milk-colored cloth and a veil of shimmering fabric so sheer I could see light through it. I tied thong sandals on my small feet. Mother had given me the clothing and asked a servant, Mia, to help me.

I had been with Jacob only two times in the company of others but trusted he was a good man. Convinced by all accounts I had nothing to fear, I put negative thoughts away. My life would be pleasant, which was all I should expect. I did not often think about the Lord, nor did I know if a woman should talk with Yahweh but I whispered, "Does our Lord look on us with favor?" Certain I would trip and fall or faint, sweat soaked my underarms. It took all the courage I had, but I stepped out of the house to walk into the warm, partly cloudy late afternoon. My knees were weak from excitement as our ceremony was to begin.

My first duty in the ritual was to walk around Jacob three times to ward off bad spirits, an old ritual handed down from nomadic kinsmen. I went through the motions of the wedding ceremony with awe and wonderment. I stole a glance at stoic Jacob and saw beads of perspiration on his forehead.

A white and yellow colored *chuppah* was set up for the ceremony. A warm breeze rippled decorative streamers of creamy white, green, and red. With the rabbi presiding, we made vows before the Lord to be faithful. Wine was poured in a small ceremonial cup to be shared. I sipped and heat rose up my neck as I grew red-faced with excitement. Jacob smashed the thin clay wine cup with his foot so we would remember how bad things sometimes happened along with the good. It was tradition. It seemed as if I were living inside a beautiful dream from which I would awaken and find myself in our vineyard crying about not having my name changed.

"Lovely," Naomi said, as she looked up with large admiring, albeit envious eyes. Her small stature gave her the appearance of childlike innocence, but I knew she was a young woman who wanted a husband and children the same as I did.

"You look very pretty, and your man is handsome."

My friend Lottie whispered in my ear, and we exchanged a private smile.

The wedding guests were joyful and ready to celebrate. Jacob's brother was drunk by the time the ceremony ended. He sauntered up to us, lost his footing. It appeared he intended to congratulate Jacob and offer a celebratory drink, but instead, he leaned in and draped an arm around my shoulder. We fell and I screamed. His weight against me was frightening and I lashed out, "Stop." Glaring angrily, Jacob swiftly helped me stand. He pulled Uzziah away, pushed him to the ground, and yelled, "Brother, have you no decency?" There was a gasp from the guests as the brothers were about to fight. Uzziah was slender and short, so Jacob could have lifted him over his shoulder with ease. He took one swing at Jacob, lost his balance, and rolled onto his side in the grass. Some guests laughed.

He grinned at Jacob, squinted. "Just wait, brother, I will get you."

Jacob shook his head and came to my side where I was dusting my garments. "Did he cause you hurt? Are you feeling all right? I am sorry for my brother's behavior. He has partaken more than enough wine." People continued their merriment, the incident forgotten.

"Meydl Tabitha, are you sure you are not hurt?" He put a protective arm around me.

"I am all right." I felt safe with my strong husband. Yet, I recalled Uzziah's threat the day we had encountered each other on the trail when I had run away from home. I worried I had not seen the last of Jacob's brother's unwanted attention.

Women set out laden trays of dates, figs, barley cakes, honey cakes, and cheese. The aroma of a fatted calf roasting on an open pit filled the air. Servants poured wine for the wedding guests. Music played on sitars and flutes wafted in the air. I felt lighthearted. People circled to dance. Jacob and I danced in the circle and twirled into the middle of it with the crowd dancing around us. Some men lifted me as if sitting in a chair and walked around with me and deposited me by Jacob. They then hoisted him up high, laughed as they made remarks about his masculine attributes. Laughter and music filled the air, and I relaxed and enjoyed the festivities. I overheard some men talking about the dispute between the brothers. "Uzziah is jealous of Jacob because he has most of his father's lands. Here is a pretty wife to make him more envious."

The weather could not have been more perfect for us and our guests. Many had come from a distance and would settle in tents nearby for the night. Food would continue to be prepared for those who stayed. Meanwhile, the meat was done and guests were eagerly assembling. When people moved away from the dance circle to the food tables as the food was being served, Jacob took my hand and led me to his house nearby.

We both touched the *mezuza* as we entered Jacob's abode with its flat roof. Our home was added on to one side of the house of Asa, where Jacob's parents and brother lived. I looked in wonder at the tidy place I would call home. There were colorful woven rugs on the floor, shelves of pots and crockery in the cooking area, a large raised bed with a brown soft fur cover in the corner of the room. I stood in the doorway quietly taking it all in. I could not quite absorb the fact it was mine.

Heat rose from my breast to my face, as I realized I was staring at our marriage bed. I wondered if he would be gentle, as I knew little about how it was with a man and a woman together. Lottie had told stories about awful experiences of newlywed women and other tales of happy coupling.

"Are you pleased?" Jacob asked. He sat and removed his sandals by the door, and I needed to take mine off as well. "Here, I will remove them for you," he said. He gestured toward the bed.

"Thank you. The place looks neat and comfortable." I sat on the bed and thought I should say more, but I was in awe of him and his surroundings. While our betrothal had been a year as prescribed, I did not know Jacob well. He was a good, successful man. His beard was trimmed and his hair, usually a mass of dark, reddish-brown curls on his head, was tamed in a tie at the nape of his thick neck.

He sat with me on our bed, looked into my eyes with dark expressive eyes, placed his arm around my waist. I felt his strength and warmth as he lifted me to his lap, and pressed my body to his. "Now, what do you think?"

"I cannot think." Although I was securely enclosed in his strong arms, I was nervous and prickles danced on my forearms. I thought I had stopped breathing for a moment.

"Do not fear me. I am to care for you as I do my own body." His eyes were half-closed as he peered at me through long dark lashes. "I have waited a long time for this day, and we are going to our marriage bed now, my beautiful wife."

"All right, Jacob," I whispered as his grip tightened around me.

He lifted and laid me gently on the soft fur and colorful covers. My veil was taken off after the ceremony. He removed my clothing one piece at a time, beginning with my embroidered sash and tunic. I did not try to help him, nor touch his clothing. He lay close and began to kiss me, lightly at first. "Your lips are sweeter than wine." His breath smelled like wine, not unpleasant. Awash in wonder, I tried to relax and let our marriage bed be what he expected. When he caressed my bare shoulders and arms, my skin tingled pleasantly. He brought my fingers to his lips, kissing them one by one, and I felt my body react in a way I had not ever experienced. Feeling moist, I whispered, "Is there anything I should do?"

And then I beheld his naked manliness. "Oh, oh, I have never seen a man's body."

"Now you have. Better for me you have not seen another. You have none to compare me with." He chuckled and reddened.

Jacob's tenderness had made our coupling go as nicely as it could. He said I was beautiful. I was no longer little Meydl; I was a woman. I experienced an inner joy thinking my loving man would be with me forever. I had hidden the cloak in a plain sack and brought it to him the morning after we were wed. "This is a gift I made for you."

"Tabitha, thank you!" He gave me a kiss and furled the cloak out to put it on.

I held my breath, hoping he would like it.

"It is a wonderful cloak, and I shall wear it everywhere." When he whirled around, I could see how nicely it suited him. He kept it on despite the warm day and wore it often.

Our life together began amiably and continued to be. Jacob worked long hours in the vineyards and fields, and I always looked forward to his return to me. I could not have been happier.

After our wedding, I asked my mother-in-law, "Would you like for me to call you Mother Menat?"

"No, Menat will do." She shrugged her shoulders and smiled. Even though our house was attached to Jacob's childhood home where his parents and brother lived, we had our privacy. Uzziah tried to make a nuisance of himself, but we ignored him. Menat called to him when she saw him come to our door and diverted his intrusion by asking him to do something.

I began to feel ill in the morning two moons after our marriage and had visions of impending peril for myself and our beautiful marriage. Any food I ate seemed destined not to remain in my stomach. Jacob, at a loss what to do, shook his head and tried to comfort me before he went out to the fields.

Five

I asked Jacob to have a servant send word to Mother. She came the next day. When I told her about my ailment, she beamed and gave me a hug. "I think you are with child, not ill. I will take care of you and answer your questions about birthing." She gave me a mint drink to ease my stomach, but I felt better having her near. It was wonderful to have a mother who was to be my midwife. Satisfied I was doing well, she left a servant, Mia, with me.

I was grateful to have Mia live with us in preparation for our firstborn. Our life was harmonious, and I was happy. The fields were similar to those I enjoyed gazing upon as a child at home. Even though some days I wanted to stay in bed when I was great with child, I walked out to the vineyard and marveled at the sight.

When the pangs of birth came upon me, Menat sent a servant to get Mother. Jacob waited with his mother. Labor took most of the day, but I forgot the pains when Mother held the wet-haired baby girl for me to see. "You did well, praise the Lord." Mother kissed my brow and laid the infant on my breast. She shone like a bright flower after a rainfall. I loved our daughter the moment I saw her.

Mother brought the swaddled baby outside to Jacob. Before he inquired about the child, he asked, "Is Meydl Tabitha doing well?"

"She is resting and has given you a beautiful girl child."

"Her name is Marian." He beamed with pleasure. We had discussed names, including Marian. He was not disappointed I had not born a son. He waited the required days and came to bed with me.

Father Asa was delighted to see a granddaughter. His health failed, and he put Jacob in charge of all his land. He gave the most to him as an inheritance when he passed away. Jacob was saddened and spent the required days of mourning and ceremony. While the family was to spend a year in grief, Jacob had little time to go through anything other than ritual. Uzziah used it as an excuse to drink and sulk.

Jacob observed the holidays and sometimes went to Jerusalem to the Temple. He traveled yearly to sell his crops. What he did not store in his bins of gleaned barley, he took to grain dealers. He had olives pressed into oil at a neighbor Azel's press. Our life together was happy, and he enjoyed playing with Marian whenever he had time. She followed him around when she began to creep and then walk. Mia sometimes had to run after her when she pushed the door open to follow her father to the fields.

I had forgotten about Uzziah's ogling because I was involved in my duties and joy as wife and mother. One day when Jacob was gone, his brother came to the well when I was drawing water. "Your arms are encrusted with fine jewels this morning. Can you spare a drink for a thirsty man?" He had come up behind me stealthily. He sounded teasing and brotherly, but his sultry eyes gave him away.

"Here," I handed him the dipper, accidentally splashed him, picked up my filled flasks and turned to go.

"What? Not even a fond kiss for your brother-in-law." He stepped in front of me.

Fear came upon me, as I remembered my encounters with him. My voice was strong and cold when I said, "I am in a hurry to get on to the work of my household." Marian, bound to my breast with a shawl, cooed and babbled. How dare he try to frighten me.

"Of course." He smiled, reached out with soft hands and touched my cheek. "A kiss from your brother." I glared angrily at him. He grinned, stepped aside. Still seething, I left apace to my door.

I wondered if I ought to tell Jacob about his brother's behavior. If Jacob knew Uzziah pestered me, he would probably beat him, or worse, so I kept quiet. I told myself no harm had been done. I would have to be mindful not to go out alone when Jacob was gone. I could have sent Mia, but I loved the chance to go outside in the fresh air.

One day I asked Jacob, "Why is Uzziah entirely different from you?"

"He was a spoiled child. My mother died when I was three. Two years later Father was attracted to Menat when he traveled afar to sell olive oil. She was small and pretty, with straight dark hair and brown eyes. He took her to be his wife, and she bore Uzziah. She doted on the boy, gave him whatever he wanted to eat. Not satisfied with his own things, he whined and once asked for a small carved camel I had. She made me give it to him and he lost it."

"I am sorry to hear how things have been between the two of you for years. My sisters and I went through a bad time, but as we grew, we became close friends. My mother died as I was born so I did not see her. Mother Erna has been good to me, and I am grateful for all she taught me. I suppose Menat may have taught you something."

"No, she paid little attention to me because I had learned how to take care of myself at a young age. Father made me his constant companion and taught me everything I know. When the time came for Father to take over Uzziah's training, there was little he could do. My brother would simply sit down and rest whenever he pleased, even when Father threatened to beat him for insolence. He would go to our mother and tell her we mistreated him. She complained to Father, who would give him a few days to rest. My brother would not change his ways. Father became more exasperated, and he hardly spoke to him. Yet one day when my brother returned after he had been gone a long time, Father was overjoyed to see him and gave him our grandfather's gold ring."

"Your father loved him."

"He did. I worried the boy would lose the ring, but he had it on his finger last time I saw. Besides Father's signet ring I have, I received something of greater value from him. I learned to work, how to handle the affairs of a household and the responsibilities of our business. I could come to the end of a day knowing I had accomplished something." Jacob tipped the cup of wine to his lips and tilted his head back, satisfied.

"You do love your work, though it is hard at times. Your father had a good partner in you."

Jacob looked up. "Father tried to impart wisdom too. He brought me to the temple in Jerusalem for festival celebrations and to learn from the rabbis there. My brother went with us when he was twelve, but he was bored and reluctant to go. In recent times when Uzziah has gone to Jerusalem, he has not been there to worship, but has been listening to Zealots, a militant group who hope to overthrow Roman rule."

"Are they dangerous? He missed a lot of good things by being stubborn."

"I do not think he is in danger. I have no love for

the Romans, but I think the Zealot group is not large enough to overtake such a widespread government. What Uzziah has not missed out on is women, music, games, and having a good time because his mother always gives him money. He drank heavily, and friends brought the useless boy home late at night. He still drinks excessively." Jacob shook his head.

"Did your father not punish him for such idle behavior?"

"He tried. When his behavior was bad enough, Menat asked Father to speak with him. Father took time away from his work in the fields during a busy harvest and asked my brother to sit and listen. He ordered him to come and work with us. We were in the middle of harvest and needed all the hands we could get. Father admonished him he would not be allowed to rest until a job was completed. He said it was time he became a man and earned his way."

"Did Uzziah work after the lecture?"

"Half-hearted. After working a short time, he wanted to have wine. I remember how Father raised his voice, 'Water is all you need. Have you seen me drink to excess? Do Jacob and I go out with our friends and stay until morning? Answer me!'"

"He had a silly grin on his face and sneered, 'No, Father, I never see you do anything to enjoy yourself.'"

"How disrespectful," I said. "It is unthinkable for a son to talk in such a way to his father."

"Father's face was flushed with anger and his fists

doubled as he told him he must earn enjoyment, not expect it. He pulled him up from the mat where he was sitting and dragged him to the field."

"Where were you all this time?"

"After listening a short while, I went to the fields to work. Father told me more details later. Uzziah came home with bleeding hands from handling dry stalks. Mother rubbed healing oil into his skin. She gave him a sack of silver coins and said she was sorry about his day."

"Were your hands bleeding?"

"No, my hands were toughened from handling sheaves for years. You and I were betrothed at the time, and my mind was on what my life would be like when we were married. I paid little heed to Uzziah. He was jealous because I had a good woman coming into my life. He assumed I would be more beloved by our father if we gave him an heir. My brother has no understanding."

"On our wedding day, I was upset by his attention."

"He tried to make it seem brotherly, but his actions were not. If he ever looks on you again, I shall kill him with my bare hands. He has always wanted what I have, but you are different than a bauble or a fine sword. You are one of a kind, my wife."

I felt much love and protection from Jacob and did not tell him of the incident at the well. I was afraid he would make good on his threat. I did not see Uzziah except at a distance for some time.

One day when I was humming a soft lullaby to Marian, a knock came on my door and Mia answered.

Uzziah was in tears, "Sister, our mother is dying." I left Marian in Mia's care.

I said nothing, although I pitied him, and sat by my mother-in-law's bed, touched her cool brow. She appeared untroubled, full lips in a bow as if asleep. Jacob draped an arm around his brother's shoulder. One could see the loss her death would bring to Uzziah's life. She died quietly, her last breath a contented sigh.

Uzziah was as one who is lost and unable to find a path. For a while, he kept to himself and did not go to town. He solaced himself with wine at home. Jacob offered to help him and put him in charge of a crew of workmen in the fields. He agreed but was a poor overseer. He arrived late to the field and left his crew to decide how to proceed without him. He tried Jacob's patience, and they argued.

"Can you lend me some coins to go to Ekron?" Uzziah pleaded.

"Loan money to you? You never pay it back, and you live in the house for no cost."

"I have every right to be in my mother's house," he said, in the voice of a petulant child.

"You have every right to work here too," Jacob yelled at him. "The slaves and I tend your portion of land for you because the crops would fail under your poor care. If you do not work, I have no use for you."

"You were always Father's favorite. He gave me

back-breaking toil to do while you got to oversee laborers." He stood, blocking the doorway, his face creased in an angry scowl.

"I have no time to discuss the past. Get out of my way." Jacob picked his brother up and shoved him outside where he landed and sat on the beaten path.

"I have friends in Jerusalem who are going to overthrow the Roman rule. One day you will be proud of me." He dusted himself off, stomped away, and was gone for weeks.

Six

Many people were ill with coughing sickness, and some died. I wanted to visit Mother and then Lottie as servants reported the illness had come upon them. I put on a cloak and started out but had such an episode of coughing I came home.

Marian and I began to cough on the same day. I felt tightness in my chest but did not go to bed because I had Marian to care for. Her fever raged. I asked Mia to fetch Mother who came and applied salve to her chest and steamed the air of our house with boiling water on the hearth. Marian improved in a few days, and I was well. Jacob became ill.

When I heard his deep cough, it was almost too much to bear. Jacob was uncomplaining and did not take to his bed in spite of my pleas. He said he had a lot of work to do. He came home in the evenings exhausted. "If I stay weary in my bones like this, we will not be able to make a son. I need one to take over for me when I am old." He smiled up at me as I bathed his fevered brow with a cool cloth.

"You will be healed soon, but you must take time. Please stop toiling hard and take one day to rest."

"I will on Sabbath, but I cannot neglect our crops and fruit. I have good hirelings, but I need to be out in the fields with them." He doubled over with a coughing spell, and I held onto his arm to guide him to his sleeping mat. I moistened the air with a kettle of boiling water on the hearth and used the salve Mother had brought. I felt blessed our daughter was well. Jacob did not completely recover but insisted it was simply a lingering cough and refused to rest.

It was time for him to take his grain and olive oil to market. He produced delicious olives, and the oil a neighbor pressed for a share. People savored our oil and paid well.

Jacob's chin was set as he reached for my hands. When he looked into my eyes, he could see I protested his going while he was feeling poorly. "I will be alright traveling and can sit and rest. Two trusted servants are with me to do all the work." His voice was strong and sounded convincing.

"It is no use trying to dissuade you. Go with the Lord watching over you," I said, and hoped the travel might revive his stamina. We grasped each other and kissed. I held onto him, but he released his arms and patted my back.

"I will return to you soon." While his face was

ashen, he sat tall on the seat as he and a servant handled the donkeys pulling the cart.

Sewing garments helped me while away the time. Lottie came to visit and played with Marian on the floor. I watched and realized how much she wanted to be a mother. She looked up at me and echoed my thoughts. "I do not know why the Lord has not blessed me with children. I have been married to Samuel for this long, and I should have at least two babies and not one has come."

"While you live a little farther away than when we first met, it is not a long walk down the trail. You may visit with my baby and future children any time you wish. Perhaps you will have children at some time, and ours can play together."

"I hope it will be so. Here you are, Marian," she said. Marian handed her the ball. The round of yarn was coming undone and she wound it tightly, tucking under the end. Marian took it and rolled it away, squealing with delight. She reached up to Lottie, smiled, patted her face, and said, "Mama."

Seven

When Jacob had been gone for several weeks, I looked for him and his servants to return every morning. I became excited as I saw someone coming down the trail, but it was not carts and servants. It was a lone man leading two donkeys with someone slouched on a donkey's back.

I ran to meet them, not sure of what I would see, but hoped there would be some word about Jacob. As the man came nearer, I saw one donkey burdened with sacks and a stack of rolled rugs on his back. I gaped in horror as I recognized my husband's cloak. He was sitting atop the donkey, slumped forward as one who is asleep.

"Someone told me this is the way to the man's home, eh."

"It is, and I am his wife. What happened? Is he. . .?" I could not form the words as I was filled with dread. Blood was encrusted on him. My head felt cold and my vision blurred. As I ran to him, I could not think and feared I would fall to the earth. "Mia!" I called to my house servant. "Come."

"He was alive when I found him on the trail. He's devoid of anything save for what's on his back. Two men lay dead nearby, eh. He needs some healing hands on his wounds. I didn't have anything to clean them save for a flask of wine, but it wasn't enough, eh. I am Zeke the Rug Man."

"Thank you, Zeke, I am Meydl Tabitha, and you have brought my husband Jacob." My dull polite words echoed as from some hollow place. My heart was screaming, and I did not want to believe what I saw and heard. I touched my husband's face and quickly withdrew my hand from his feverish brow as from a fire. His illness had become worse. In a blur, I saw servants rush in from our nearby vineyard. Zeke led the donkey close to the front door of the house, where two servants lifted Jacob down, laid him on a woven rug, and carried him into the house to his bed. My feeling was as if I had eaten something spoiled. My mind was filled with many thoughts, and I could not think of what to do next. Mia covered Jacob and stood by waiting for me to dismiss her or tell her what to do. The servants, Sheaf and Moor, nodded and went on to work.

"Jacob, oh Jacob, what happened? Speak to me." I began to sob in spite of my will to remain calm. "Mia, bring water." Mia went to the kitchen to get the ewer of water and clean rags to wash his face. I took a wet cloth and began to cleanse and rub balm into his wounds to soothe him. Mia stood near me with a fresh cloth.

"Meydl, do you need my help, eh?" Zeke stood respectfully. He said my name with a lilting accent, May-dell, and it sounded pleasant. Marian, our daughter, came running in from outside.

"Is Papa home? Who is the man in the turban?"

"Yes, Papa is home, but he is not well. Be a good girl and show this nice man where the well and trough are as he and his donkeys need water. They brought him home." I wanted to clean the blood off Jacob's face and clothes before Marian got a good look at him.

"Yes, Mother," she said.

"We will do fine here, Rug Man. Thank you for your kindness. Please stay for food."

"There is no need." He turned to Marian, "I am Zeke the Rug Man, and what is your name, young girl?"

"Marian, and I will soon be six. I know the way to the well. It is over by those trees, so come with me." She skipped outside and Zeke followed, smiling.

I cleansed Jacob's wounds, rubbed them with healing salve, and bound the worst ones. I put my lips to my husband's forehead and kissed him. "Jacob," I whispered, but he did not answer. He was breathing, and I could feel his life pulse beating. I used water to cool his feverish face and limbs, hoping and praying he would recover.

I heard Zeke coming after a while and called to him, "Come inside if you want."

"You have a smart little daughter. She showed me the well and then went off to play in the shade of the house. Thank you for the water, and I was pleased there was a trough for my donkeys, eh."

"Yes, happy you could refresh yourself. Would you like some bread? How can I ever repay you?" I left Mia to attend Jacob, and I went to the stone jar where I kept coins and started to take some out.

"No, I can't take your money. I was on the trail selling wares myself, and it could've happened to me. Your man would've done the same if I'd been hurt, eh."

"He would." I went to get a round of bread, and Zeke shook his head.

"No, I can't take time for a sup. I must be on my way. Is there anything you need, eh? I have a new soft sleeping rug to help him rest."

"How kind of you to think of his comfort. I thank the Lord for you." I wanted to repay this man with the graying beard. "Yes, I will buy it."

Zeke brought the sleeping mat inside the house and unrolled it to put it on Jacob's bed. He helped Mia move Jacob to lie down on its softness. "I have a way to go by day's end," he said. Mia handed him the round of bread.

"Thank you." He tucked it into his cloth bag.

"You have done much for me, yet I do not know what happened. Can you tell me anything?"

"Yes, the earth was disturbed by a struggle, and there were cartwheel and donkey tracks. I'd say your husband must've been coming home from selling his grains or something and had money on him. Thieves attacked them, I'd say. Left them all for dead, but your man stayed alive, eh."

"By the grace of YHWH."

It was a day in late fall and the air was crisp and dry. As we stepped outside, I heard bugs buzzing about. Zeke started to walk away when I wondered, "How did you know where to bring Jacob?"

"Since the man did not speak, eh, I traveled the direction he was probably going by following this familiar trail."

"Are you sure Mia cannot give you more food?"

"No, thank you, the bread is enough. I hope the good man comes out of it." Zeke went away, leading his donkeys.

"I showed him the well, and I waved to him when he left." Marian skipped in behind me as I came inside. "Can I see Papa now?"

"Yes, but be quiet as he is asleep."

She tiptoed to him and blew a kiss, then went to play with a ball of yarn she rolled across the floor. "I will be quiet," she whispered.

"Thank you, sweet Marian." I gave my full attention to Jacob. For the first few days he would not speak, only sigh or nod his head. "Here is some broth for you." I offered a spoonful to his parched lips, but he kept his mouth closed and shook his head once from side to side. Days passed.

"Drink some water, Papa." Our daughter Marian had a cup in her hand and a worried frown on her little face. Her wavy brown tresses shone with gold highlights as the sunbeams from the window touched her. He opened his eyes and tried to smile. When she put the rim of the cup to his lips, he took a sip of water. Her brown eyes beamed with love and she smiled. "Papa, you need water. Drink some more." He patted her head and closed his eyes. Marian sat and played quietly. At night, she went to her bed and did not disturb us or ask for anything. I was pleased with her, as it allowed me to give my full attention to Jacob.

I made a fresh salve of herbs and fat for his wounds and Mia rewrapped them with clean cloths. As night fell, he expelled a deep resounding cough, and I gave him syrup of honey and wine to help relieve it. He accepted it as well as sips of water and wine. His brow was hot to my touch. As he moaned in his sleep, I kept a vigil through the night. I bathed his arms with a cool wet cloth.

I went to the field beside the well to find the plant I hoped would bring relief from his fever. I had brewed the last cup of tea from the dried willow bark I had on my shelf. I looked up as I plucked the herb leaves because I heard Uzziah approach. "My brother is ill?"

"Yes. I trust you will do his share of work while he is abed." I stood and looked him in the eye. "Did you hear what happened to him?"

Uzziah stopped, did not meet my eyes when he

spoke. "The hirelings say he had a lingering cough."

"Yes, he had coughing sickness but went to sell grain anyway. When he and two servants were returning home from selling the grain, they were attacked. Thieves killed and robbed them. Jacob is fortunate to be alive. A kind old rug peddler brought him home."

"What dreadful news. I shall go in to see him."

"I do not know where you have been, but you should have gone to sell the harvested grain and olive oil and left your brother home as he was not well." I turned away, disgusted with irresponsible Uzziah.

"What?" His lip curled, he sneered. "What right have you to speak with me, woman? You know Jacob would not have trusted me to sell grain or anything." He shook his fist in the air, walked from the well to our house, and went inside. I did not follow him because I did not want to upset Jacob by arguing with Uzziah. I was glad I found the plant and bent to pluck the leaves I needed to relieve Jacob's pain and fever.

As I approached my door, Uzziah came out shaking his head. When I went inside, Jacob's clothing was soaked with sweat and his woolen coverlet tossed aside. His eyes were closed and he was quiet. I rushed to him and was relieved he breathed and felt warm, not hot, to my touch.

One gloomy day followed another. Even with Mia's help, I grew extremely tired ministering to my sick husband but did not give in to weariness. My heart ached with longing for the life we had before. Nothing was the same since the coughing illness came and afflicted many slaves and neighbors. And now Jacob seemed to be nearing his deathbed. I sent a servant to get word to my mother.

I was stirring a soup at the hearth thinking of what else I could do to bring him comfort when Jacob opened his eyes and in a clear voice called, "Tabitha."

"Jacob, you have awakened." I felt excited because he spoke. I knelt beside him and smoothed his brow. "You have had nothing except small spoons of broth and drops of water on your tongue. I have a rich barley soup with many vegetables I will bring to you."

"Tabitha, beloved." Jacob reached up to my face and caressed it with his rough hand. He coughed, and I helped him sit to make it easier. His brow was warm to the touch.

"Are you feeling better?" I propped a cushion behind his back. Mia brought him a bowl of soup and a round of bread. A pink color slowly returned to his swollen discolored face with each spoonful of soup he fed himself. I felt a light-heartedness and hope.

"Was my cloak stolen or ruined?" His voice was hoarse.

"I washed and mended it, but some stains I could not remove. It is ready for you to wear." My hands had chafed when I scrubbed the dried bloodstains with stone and sand.

"Thank you." His face brightened, yet a furrowed brow was ever present. The hopelessness in Jacob's voice broke my heart. He paused for a long time, and I thought he slept. Then he said, "I feel useless and weak. I am not fit to be a man, much less a husband and property owner." His breath came in gasps. "How can I do anything when I am like this?" The utter despair showed on his countenance as he settled his large frame, grown thin and bony.

"Only for a time, Jacob. Soon you will be out in the fields again." The aroma of lamb and vegetable stew filled the air.

"Papa, you can give me a kiss," Marian said, smiling.

"Come," he said. "How old is Marian?"

"Six, Papa, but not old enough for you to get me a husband." She grinned a coy smile and shrugged.

He smiled. "Come closer." He motioned to me with his hand. I went to him and he caught Marian and me in a warm embrace.

In the evening when he drifted off to sleep, I prayed, "Lord, I know I am a mere woman and should not speak, yet I plead. Please grant healing to Jacob, and give us patience."

Next morning, he lay still. Was this the way the Lord answered my prayer? I touched his hand and found it was cold. Dread seized me when I bent next to his face and felt no breath coming from his nostrils or mouth. How was it he lived and breathed yesterday, and in an instant today he was not here?

The warmth of our passions lingered in my heart and mind. It did not seem real he was gone, and I pinched my arm hard to make sure this was not an awful dream. I gave in to great racking sobs, then I cried softly, thinking of what needed to be done, and Marian.

Marian was the one bright star in my world. She walked beside me the day after the funeral and burial procedures had all been completed. "I am happy you are with me, and also Grandmother, Aunt Phoebe, and Aunt Lottie." Marian hugged me tightly, and I bent down to hold her in my arms. "I am going to go in the shade of the house and hold my baby doll Aunt Phoebe gave me." She skipped away.

I was glad Marian had accepted her father would not be coming back to us. Many random thoughts crossed my mind as I walked among the vines in our small vineyard. I noted a few late purple grapes were dry and shriveling. Some diligent slave had weeded these nearest the house. I tried to think about practical work to be done with the crops. A feeling of dread stopped me as if I had walked into a tree trunk. By law, after his death, all of Jacob's possessions belonged to Uzziah. As much as I disliked the man, I would be his brother's wife. I shuddered and wanted to flee from my fate. Where could I go?

"Dear Yahweh . . ." I tried to pray, but no words came. I gazed down along the pathway and saw a length of natural colored thread that dangled from a grapevine. It appeared to have flown in on a wind. I tugged on it, wondered how it had come to be in this place. I yanked more, but it did not loosen or break free. On closer examination, I found it was three thin strands twisted together. I had never seen such fine thread. From whence had it come? Was it unbreakable? Was there any such thing?

I gazed at our harvested vineyard as I turned and slowly walked to our house with lingering thoughts of my past, both good and bad times. Now I faced the present. My life had changed forever.

Eight

Uzziah! As distasteful to me as it was, he was legally obligated to be my husband since his brother died. My stomach was ill with the thought of marriage to a mean, lazy boy, disguised as a man.

We had sat together all week and greeted visitors who came to sit in honor of the dead and mourn with us. I feared the worst but hoped Uzziah's new responsibility would make him grow up. We were to observe the required seven days of mourning before we came together. I had hoped he would wait the full year.

On the eighth day, I met him outside, and boldly asked, "Must we be together as husband and wife? Can we pretend to be married as prescribed by law, but not in private?"

"Meydl, I laugh at the suggestion. You are my wife, and I will enjoy spending my first night in your loving embrace. I have longed for you since I was a boy, and now you are mine. You are sure to enjoy what I have for you." He patted his tunic below his stomach and had a sultry look on his face.

I was disgusted, felt ill in my stomach and turned away embarrassed. He waited another few days and then approached me. He had called me Meydl, and I resented him not using Tabitha, but said nothing.

"The time has come for you to take off your black robes and put on light garments for the marriage bed."

"As you have said," I answered coldly. I wanted to escape as I was not ready for him, and I never would be. "Our union is not blessed."

"It is decreed by law, and we must do it for Jacob." The lilt of his voice was unmistakable, lustful, his facial expression cold under the cover of doing the right thing. I felt nothing but contempt for him.

Our first evening together, he asked Mia to take Marian to Lottie's home to spend the night. He had another hireling make a fine meal of roasted lamb meat, bread, herbs, and red wine. A lamp lighted the cloth as we reclined, eating succulent grapes and drinking red wine in my home, Jacob's home.

I was tense with dread and I grieved over the loss of my husband and I wanted to delay intimacy with Uzziah. I made an excuse to get up and go outside for a moment. I looked toward the heavens, begging the dark starry sky to take me away. "Lord, must I do this? I have no heart for this man." The sky clouded, snuffing out stars as if to reflect my feelings. So much for trying to pray, I thought. I dreaded becoming Uzziah's wife. It was what I was expected to do, but I hated it.

He called to me, "Come, I cannot believe my good fortune. My eyes forever have made love with your beauty. I may not be as tall as my brother, yet I will not disappoint you. We will go to my bed in our house after we have supped."

He held my arm, guided me to his door. Reluctantly, I came inside his deceased mother's home where I had been more of a guest than family. It was now my home, but in my heart, I was an outsider. I sat on a soft red cushion, quietly sipping wine. The air smelled stale, like old clothing stored away. I could not imagine how this was mine. When the clay goblet was empty, I said, "Please pour more wine for me." I needed the mellow feeling it gave in order to at least pretend to enjoy his company. Never had I overindulged in wine, but I wanted to now, and he gave me another half goblet. I took deep swallows and finished it. He took both my hands and helped me up.

He held my arm and walked me to his bed. Perhaps it was the wine, but I was surprised at how carefully he treated me at first, and how he caressed and loved me with practiced hands. I thought he must have enjoyed many hours with other women. After he was spent and asleep, I left the bed to go wash. While I would have liked to have another baby, I did not want to have his child.

Our life, while not ideal, was tolerable for a time.

Uzziah did not work the fields as Jacob had done but put hirelings in charge of the slaves. He rarely went to oversee them. Instead, he demanded my attention and sometimes had Marian and Mia stay with neighbor Lottie. Then he delighted in using Jacob's bed. He became rough in his play with my body, rubbing until I chafed and sometimes flipped me over to spank my bare behind. When I cried and begged him to stop, he turned a deaf ear. After a few weeks of pleasuring himself with me, he grew bored and left me in our bed one morning. I had refused him the previous evening, begging my time of the moon cycle.

He did not tell me how many days he would be away. I was relieved he was gone but worried he would return drunk in the evening. I asked Mia to take Marian to Lottie and Samuel for the night in case there was trouble. He arrived long after dark, and I met him at the door with my arms folded across my chest. "Why were you out late?"

"What kind of question do you ask?" Uzziah slurred.

"A wife's question." I grabbed a staff and blocked the doorway, determined not to let him in.

"Ah, you missed me and want me."

"No, stay out of Jacob's house." I smelled the strong drink on his breath and wanted no part of him. I stood at the door, muscles taut, ready to run if necessary. "Go to your home and sleep."

"My house then, but you will come with me." His face was blotched red. He picked up and threw a clod of dirt through the open doorway. It spattered a wall across the room and distracted me.

He shoved me aside and I stumbled, sat on the floor. He came in, fell on the bed, and beckoned to me with his hand. When I stood but did not move, he sprang up and grabbed me. When I wriggled out of his grasp, he swung at me with his open hand and slapped my face. It hurt, but I did not cry. I felt helpless. I was his wife and by law, he could punish me.

"Now, come to me," he commanded.

I sidestepped him, but not fast enough. He lunged toward me, threw me to the floor. Pain permeated my being, and I could not move. He took me forcibly as I lay on the hard-packed dirt floor. I sobbed, hurt and humiliated.

When I awakened chilled, it was dark, and he was gone. Everything else seemed normal, and I heard a night bird twittering outside. I got up, cleansed my body and dressed. When it was daylight, I checked his house and he was not there. I went to get Marian from Lottie's house.

I hoped Uzziah would not return, but he did. "How is my beautiful wife?" He kissed me lightly and behaved as if nothing bad had happened. He was the same lazy man and did not look after the hirelings or crops. Within a week he went away for days, returned home to demand my attention. Whenever I refused, he hurt me, so I unwillingly succumbed.

"You must start managing the hirelings and the

crops," I said. "We are in the midst of a dry spell and there are steps you should take to prepare for the worst." I tried to instruct him, but my words were wasted. I sorely missed Jacob, his kind treatment of me, and his expert management of crops and hirelings.

"What can I do about the dry earth when no rain falls? Shall I ask the desert gods to bring a flood upon our land?" Uzziah scoffed, "Even your beloved Jacob could not control the weather."

"Only Lord God can command or withhold rain." I turned from him without further speech. He grabbed me and kissed me so hard my lips bled. He shoved me aside and I stumbled. He took a sack of money from my small brown kitchen crock and walked out the door.

"When will you return home?" I called after him and dabbed at my lip with a cloth. I knew it was wrong, but I prayed he would not return.

Nine

I fled to the doorway, terrified when I awakened to smoke in the air. I rushed back inside to grab sleepy Marian. Mia woke up. "Come! We must get out of here." Hungry flames licked a wall beside my daughter's bed.

"What is happening?" Marian asked, rubbing her eyes.

"Fire! A fire is destroying everything. Hurry!"

"I need this!" She picked up her sewing basket. "My tunic."

"All right, but do not tarry."

"My thread broke when last I stitched," she shrieked.

"We can take care of it later." We ran as fast as we could away from hungry flames as they devoured my thatched roof like a ravenous animal.

I felt sick at heart as we ran on the trail to Lottie and Samuel's home. Marian was crying.

"I saw the smoke billowing in the air." Lottie, running, met us on the trail. "Was it your home?" She looked frightened.

"Yes." I collapsed in her arms and held Marian's hand.

"What do you suppose caused it?" Lottie looked at me, concerned.

Marian cried uncontrollably and when I comforted her, she stopped sobbing enough to say, "Could it have been the candle I left burning when I could not sleep?"

I wrapped my arms around her and we wept together. "We will build a new home, Marian," I said, but I did not know how I would accomplish it.

Samuel came running and continued toward the fire where he stayed for a time. He returned to us and sadly shook his head. "There is not enough water to put out the fire, and it has done much damage." Later in the day we all went to see the result and found the outdoor oven untouched, but nothing else was left among the smoldering embers except the toppled clay bricks, a small gray mass, and charred crockery. The attached home of Father Asa and Menat was reduced to stubble and ash with a large square of burnt bricks standing as a reminder of its size. While Uzziah had insisted we should do so, I had not wanted to occupy their house after Jacob died. I asked him to wait awhile. Now I never would.

I was at a loss of what to do. Both of my sisters had married. Mother was busy taking care of Father.

I thought I could go there to help if they needed me. Marian, Mia, and I walked with Lottie and Samuel to their house. We sat drinking water.

"Come live with us for now," Lottie said. Samuel nodded in agreement.

"I appreciate your kindness more than I can express." I looked to Samuel who stood by us.

"We have room for you." Samuel pointed to a place we could roll out sleeping mats next to the kitchen hearth. "I have enough soft floor rugs for you."

I was grateful for my good friends. I refused to think of what might happen when Uzziah returned to find he was homeless.

Marian sat outside Lottie's house and worked on the tunic she had saved. I was inside helping Lottie and Mia prepare vegetables for a stew when my daughter called, "Mother, I need your help."

I wiped my hands and came out to breathe in the cool air on a sunny day. I looked at the plain tan tunic she held up. "It looks beautiful," I said.

"My tunic would be prettier with embroidered flowers. Will you please teach me?"

"You have done nice work." I turned it inside out to admire her stitching. "Embroidery is not difficult and I think you could master it, but I fear we do not have the right colored threads in your basket."

"I am sorry," Marian said, and bowed her head.

"Why?" I put my arms around her.

"I do have many colors of thread I took from your

basket some days before the fire, and I did not tell you. I meant to let you know but did not ask first. I think I am a thief." She brought out coiled threads of green, brown, yellow, and red.

"Marian." I breathed a sigh of relief, yet thought I should admonish her not to take something without asking. I did not know what else to do and sat with her enfolded in my arms as she sniffled. At last, I said, "You are forgiven for taking the thread, and please do not do it again. If you had asked, I would have let you have it. I will start teaching you embroidery." I gently tapped her hand she put in front of me, and we both smiled and set to work.

"Mother, are we going to build a new home? I can see you miss it, as you are sad-faced. I like Lottie and Samuel, but it would be nice to have a place of our own."

"I do not know, but I trust we will find a way. The Lord takes care of us, and I am sure he has a plan." I wondered if I spoke empty words but wanted to give my daughter hope. A couple of days later, Samuel surprised me as we sat to sup the evening meal.

"We do like having you here, but would you consider building a small place of your own where your house stood?" Samuel looked at me with his kind, earnest eyes. The spicy aroma of Lottie's lamb stew filled the air. Her face encouraged me without words.

"Yes, I would like to rebuild, but I do not know how to begin. I worry I will not be able to do it at all, yet do not want to give up. The oven is still there, some bricks remain, but it needs something other than a bit of thatch to cover it," I said. Mia filled our cups with wine. Marian nibbled on a piece of bread and looked up at me with smiling eyes.

"We can help. Our neighbor James, beyond the hill to the south of us, was going to build a shed for his milk goats but has decided instead to keep only one nanny. He may give us a good price on materials, and I think he will sell an extra milk goat."

I was overwhelmed by everyone's kindness. "Much more than a neighbor should ever expect. I would appreciate it, and feel humbled by his generosity."

"I miss you already, but I know you do want your own place." Lottie sopped her bread into the stew and looked up, satisfied.

In a few days, Samuel and James came with carts of sunbaked brick, a few pieces of wood and thatch. The two men used a plumb line and began to construct a hut, using most of the remaining brick. It was to be one room with an earthen floor and thatch roof. Marian and I went there daily to watch the progress and bring the men water from the well. Mia put bread in our oven to bake and brought it out for the workers to eat. I felt truly blessed.

When the house was finished, it smelled faintly of the charred brick. I had a small kitchen area with two shelves for dishes. Beneath the shelf was room for a flour bin and oil cruze. In one corner was a shelf to hold clothing, and beneath the shelf was a place for our baskets of sewing supplies. I vowed to buy a new sewing basket soon. Lottie had given me three rolled mats we brought out every night for sleeping. A small oil lamp, a gift from Naomi, I put on the floor in the center of the room. I looked at my hut with satisfaction. It was not as grand as my former home, but there was enough room for Marian, Mia, and me. The nanny goat was tethered outside until we could build her a small cover. I felt cozy and sheltered and was lulled into feeling secure.

My safety was torn apart some months later when Uzziah burst in unannounced. He roared, "What did you do to the house? I leave for a little while and come home to this small hut. It is no wonder I stay away. You do not take care of the home I provide for you. My father's house is gone." His rant made him breathless, voice slurred, and he staggered.

"You have not provided a home, and I am sorry the house burned down. Did you ever worry about us? Marian and I are fortunate to be alive." I turned away from him, furious. I knew he would not listen to reason, so I said no more, and he was too drunk to continue. I unrolled a mat for him, and he dropped down onto it and fell into a snoring sleep. I grasped Marian's hand without a word, and to Mia, I said, "Come, let us go to Lottie and Samuel's place before it is completely dark."

Stars were out as I knocked. "Lottie!" My chest was drumming, and my breath was like an animal panting.

"What is it?" Lottie opened her door holding a

small lamp in her hand. "Are you ill? How can I help?"

"We need a safe place to sleep for the night."

"Oh, my friend." Lottie embraced me, kissed both tear-stained cheeks.

"Thank you," I said. Marian and Mia quietly followed me inside.

"He came back." Samuel's voice was drowsy. "Is there something I need to do for you tonight?"

"Yes, Uzziah is home, and thank you, both. I am sorry to disturb you as you are settling for the night. Please go on to sleep."

Lottie put some soft rugs and blankets on the floor for us and asked no further questions. "Sleep well. You can tell me everything in the morning." She went to lie down beside Samuel.

I did not sleep but tossed and turned. I hoped Uzziah would not follow us when he awakened. He was my husband and could do what he wanted with me. I was fearful he would beat me. No authority would punish him for mistreating his wife. All he had to say was I disobeyed him. I wanted to flee far away but had no place I could go. I thought of my mother whose home was on the same trail in the opposite direction, but I did not want to trouble her or my sisters. Uzziah knew where they lived. Tears dried on my face as I pondered my situation, and sleep would not come.

In the morning, I told Lottie what had happened and asked if Marian could stay with her. Lottie was delighted to have Marian. "It will only be for a short while," I said, and hoped it was true.

"She can stay as long as she wants." Lottie wrapped a protective arm around my daughter. "I wish I had a way to protect you too."

When I returned to my hut later in the morning, accompanied by Mia, I was relieved Uzziah was not there. Once more, he stayed away, yet I dreaded he would return to hurt me.

The barley harvest was the least yield it had ever been, and the olive trees bore small fruit. There would be less oil to press. Tax collectors came and wanted to speak with my husband. I told them my husband was dead. It was at least half true. They offered condolence but taxed my small grain harvest and there was little left to sell. I stored small crocks of grain for my own use to grind into flour for bread.

An uneventful year passed. As I sat in front sewing, something happened to the thread. It became entangled and when I tried to sort it out, the thread came apart. How I wished for unbreakable thread and wondered if such a thing was possible. Whenever I could, I was determined to seek and find it.

I stood and saw the approach of a horse-drawn chariot raising dust on the trail in the distance. I was thankful Marian was with Lottie and Samuel. My heart pounded in fear, but I did not retreat into my hut.

A man, dressed in a fine dark brown cloak, climbed nimbly from the chariot. His servant sat with the reins in his hands as if ready to dash away at a moment's notice. The official had a parchment roll in his hand as he walked toward Mia, who stood beside me. "Is the landowner here? I have business with him." His voice was hoarse, authoritative, and his dark eyes pierced mine from beneath his bushy black eyebrows.

"He is not here. Who are you?" I thrust my shaking hands into my tunic folds, stepped forward, and stared boldly at the hook-nosed man. This time I did not lie. Uzziah was my husband.

"I am Saul, come to collect tax owed to Caesar. I must speak with the landowner. When will he return?" Saul moved closer to me and thrust the rolled document toward me like a weapon.

"I cannot say." I frowned, willed my voice to stay strong. "You can state your business to me."

"I have no proof of your status, woman." He hesitated, suspicious eyes probed. As if speaking to a slave or one who has no sense, he repeated, "I have come to collect taxes from the landowner." His hand relaxed in front of him. "Ask the coward to come out of the house."

"He is not in the house. The crops produced scant yield, and I have no money. Please go away."

"Your husband has property," Saul sneered. "We will confiscate the land if he does not pay his taxes." His thin lips bowed into a false, leering smile.

"Surely not everything. Where will I live?" The words came out in a half-whisper. "What shall we eat?"

"Oh, we don't care about your little hut or your milk goat," he said and gestured toward the tethered nanny standing by her small shelter. His voice changed from benevolent to menacing. "Your husband will no longer have use of the land."

"You cannot take everything." I forced myself to remain calm and not cry. The air was stifling, dry, and my lips were cracked and burned. I paused. "All of it?"

"Yes." Saul did not flinch or weaken.

"But we have had a severe drought. Everyone's land is like our own. Can you give us another year's time?" I bit my sore lip.

The man did not answer but turned away, hopped up, and sped off in his horse-drawn chariot. I flung my arm up protectively as the wheels spewed fine sand and gravel which spattered and stung my face and arms.

I watched them leave as questions filled my mind. What would happen to our hirelings and servants? My goat could provide milk and cheese as it was able to graze on the sparse stubble, but was it still mine? I had barley meal to last for one winter, two flasks of wine and stone jars of olive oil.

I called to Mia, who was pouring some of the goat's milk into an ox bladder to make cheese. "I do not know how to tell you. You have always been a good worker for us and have done nothing wrong."

"You need not say a word. I will miss you, but I will find another household." She knew my situation and bowed, submissive and respectful.

"To whom will you go?"

"Back to your mother or your neighbor Lottie."

"I do hope Mother or Lottie will have you." I embraced Mia and let her go. The next day when I walked to the servant's huts to let them free, I found no sign of them or their things. They had left in the night without a word because they did not want to be slaves to the Romans.

One of my father's servants came riding on a horse. He alit and gave me sad news. "Your father died peacefully. Your mother wants you to come."

Mia and I went to see Mother, and Phoebe was with her. Naomi and her husband arrived. We all cried together and prepared Father's body for burial in a cave. Ritual washing was done by all of us who had been with his body. Other neighbors joined in the funeral as we laid him to rest. We observed the seven days of mourning together.

"Mother, I wish I could bring you home to live with me, but I have such a small hut and my daughter spends most of her days with Lottie."

"Do not concern yourself with me. I am glad you and Lottie have remained friends."

"She is my best friend. I do want to help you, Mother."

"All will be well." Mother patted my arm. "Naomi is with child and has asked me to come live with them. Phoebe and her husband live near Naomi, so you and Marian must come and stay awhile."

"I am glad the tax collectors did not take your

property," I said.

Sadness creased Mother's face and she looked away. "I believe they hastened your father's death. We have our home and there is a small field for our barley crops." Mother put her scarf to her face and wept. "They took the rest."

I held her close. We wept together over many sorrows.

I went home after a few days. As I walked, the gloom of a clouded sunless sky was a twin to my grief. I agonized and wondered where our God was when everything seemed to be going wrong in my life. As a mere woman, I doubted my prayers were heard.

How would I face the winter without any land or crops to harvest?

Ten

I sat in the shade of my hut absorbed in my sewing, and I was startled as I saw on the trail a gentleman wearing a faded red turban and colorful clothing. He led a donkey laden with rolled carpets and fabrics. "Good day, woman, I was wondering if you could give a traveler a drink of water, eh."

I recognized him. "Good day to you, Zeke the Rug Man. I do not own the well, a stone's throw away, but you may help yourself. It is open to anyone."

After he had gone to the well, he came to the shade of the hut. "You do remember me, eh?" He sat down.

"How can I forget you saved my husband's life and brought him here? Sadly, he did not recover and died." I sat on the ground, clasped my hands together around my bent knees and long tunic, and talked with him. I did not get many visitors, and it was a custom to offer hospitality to all who came to one's door. His company was a pleasant distraction.

"Sad to hear your good man died." His voice was sincere. When I nodded, he paused and gestured toward his donkey. "I sell wares if you remember. I can give you a good price on fine cloth for a new cloak, eh?"

"I do sew, but cannot buy anything because I have little money. I would like thread with which to sew, an unbreakable thread."

Zeke shook his head, chuckled. "If you ever find such a fine thread, let me know. There's many would buy it, eh." He paused, waited for my response, then said, "Something happened here, eh?"

"Yes, a fire, and I lost my property to Roman taxes." I was disquieted as if I tasted something bitter, and I am sure it showed on my face.

"The tax collectors are scoundrels." A wind began to pick up and toss chaff about, and a light rain began to fall.

"I cannot deny it." The raindrops felt refreshing after being without moisture for so long. I did not rise to move into the house, and Zeke did not seem to mind getting wet.

"You are a widow, eh? It's a hard life alone." He tucked a stray strand of gray hair into his faded crimson turban and looked off in the distance. "They took your home?"

"No, it was an accidental fire." I did not know how to respond, because I did not want him to feel sorry for me. We sat in silent companionship for a time, watching the rain come down.

"Will you and the daughter be all right? Is the child asleep?" He squinted at me as he faced the setting sun. More gray hair escaped his turban and framed his face. The shower moved on, and we had a few fluffy clouds.

"She and my servant are with my neighbor, and I am managing here. You must leave soon. It becomes like the dark of the blind when there is a tiny sliver of moon in the sky." I would have liked for him to stay but did not think it would be proper.

Zeke stood and offered a hand to help me up. "I'll be off then, eh." He led his donkey down the trail. I waved, smiled thinking of Zeke's visit as it had taken me away from my sorrows for a brief time.

Many moons had waxed and waned since Uzziah had been home, and I hoped I would never see him again. But one day, there he was.

Eleven

s I saw Uzziah striding toward me, I had to force myself to gain control of my impulse to run. I dropped the tunic I was making into my sewing basket and rose from sitting outside my hut. His hair was dull and fell in mats about his shoulders. He had grown fat and had a long beard, but it was unmistakably him.

"Good day," he slurred.

"What brings you home?" My eyes blinked as I tried to get used to his new appearance. I was repulsed. His belly bulged his tunic tight across his middle like a nanny goat about to give birth, but his brown ankles betrayed legs thin as sticks.

"Drought has hurt the barley. It looks bad." He stated the obvious and flopped down on the low stool I had been sitting on. He patted the earth beside him, expecting me to sit.

"It matters not there is no crop." I wanted no part

of this man and wished for a way to rid myself of him.

"Why do you say such a thing?" He continued to idly pat the air above the ground.

"We no longer own the land." He had not even noticed the absence of workers.

"You cannot have sold it without me." He squinted, trying to sort out what I had said. His hands curled into fists, and he glared. "Last time I came back to a hut instead of my home because you were careless and burned the place down. Now I return home and the property . . ." He raised his voice and his fist, and lowered it, snarling, "You are the worst wife a man could have. My means of making a living gone because of you." He stood and glowered.

"No. The Romans took it for taxes." I made my voice stony and wiped away unshed tears with my fingertips. "Had you been here, perhaps you could have reasoned with them."

"Where are all the servants? I would not have let the tax collector s have it."

"Do you think I gave your father's land to them? The servants left." I spoke, emphasizing each word. I looked him in the eye until he turned his face away.

"Why are you still here?" He blinked, and his voice had toned down.

"The officials left me the house, oven, and milk goat, and the water well is available for all to use."

He continued to avoid my gaze and did not ask me about Marian. "Now, what am I going to do?" he whined.

I smiled, ready to tell him he would do whatever it was he had always done, but I was afraid he would beat me for an insolent answer. I stood waiting for him to say more. The air had stilled and the sun seemed hotter than usual. "Shall we go to the well and get you a drink of cool water?"

"Yes, I would like for you to bring me some water." He sat again, breathing heavily as if from exertion.

I rushed to the well, glad for the chance to decide what I was going to say or do next. I paused to think, wondered if he would follow me if I walked away and kept going.

When I came into my hut, he was sprawled on the bedding. I poured a cup of water from the flask and gave it to him. He had not removed his sandals. My wifely impulse was to go to him, take them off, and bathe his travel-worn feet. I thought he could not find fault with me for doing so. When I knelt by him with a basin of water, he reached for me and began yanking my hair.

"Stop. I brought your water. Stop!" I screamed, trying to wrench myself out of his clutches, but he was stronger and heavier. While he pulled me onto the bed by my hair, his other arm wrapped around my body and forced me to lie with him.

"Water is not all a man needs after his travels," he said in a husky voice.

I knew I had no defense against him, as he was my husband. I meekly submitted, even as his foul odor nauseated me. I hoped I would spew bile on Uzziah. I loathed him.

When he fell asleep, I dressed and went outside to retrieve my sewing basket and stool. The sun was setting, and the first star of the night began to beam its light. It all seemed so ordinary, but my life was not. Hunger gnawed at my stomach, and I went inside to eat some cheese, bread, and figs. I drank a cup of the water I had drawn earlier. There was no wine in the hut, and if there had been, I knew Uzziah would drink it. In desperation, I whispered, "I am a woman and should not speak, yet Lord, please help me."

There had to be a way to escape my horror and sorrow, but I did not know how. I had a useless and violent husband, little food, and no source of income. Pride kept me from begging from family, or anyone. It was enough Lottie had agreed to take care of my daughter. Marian would soon be old enough for marriage. Samuel and Lottie could find a good husband for her. I had a wonderful friend and a darling daughter. I would not endanger their lives by going there tonight.

I thought of walking in the dark all the way to my mother's house farther down the trail past Lottie's home but was too tired to move. I put a sleeping mat on the floor on the opposite side of the hut from him and slumbered fitfully. When day dawned, I was hoping he would be gone, but he was there, snoring. I went outside to milk the goat and give her water. The little nanny was gentle, a sweet gray and white goat with long hair. I patted her on the head after I finished milking.

Inside my hut, I poured some milk into a storage crock for later and put half of it into an ox bladder to make cheese. I was thankful. "The Lord has left me with something to eat. Maybe it is all I need."

Uzziah stirred, rolled over, and remained asleep. I watched him and was glad for a short reprieve. If he beat me, I would leave but did not know where I would go. Perhaps Lottie would have an idea. When I finished sweeping the hut, I walked to her house. I longed to see my daughter.

Marian met me at the door and wrapped her arms around me. Lottie was right behind her, and we embraced and kissed cheeks.

"How are you doing?" I asked.

"Very well, Mother. Lottie is teaching me to weave." Marian rushed to the corner of the room to show me the small lap loom on which she had set the warp of natural cotton thread to weave a scarf.

"It is going to be beautiful, and I am proud of you." I turned to Lottie. "Thank you for doing this for me."

"Marian is a delightful girl. I enjoy teaching as much as she does learning. And tell me about yourself. Are you not lonely these days?"

"Oh, I am all right." I hesitated to tell her about Uzziah's return, but my friend knew something was amiss from the look in my eyes.

"Come outside," Lottie brightened. "I want to show you some herbs I have been growing. Marian, please finish helping Mia with the dishes."

When we stepped out, I whispered, "Uzziah is here."

"Now what will you do?"

"I want to go a great distance from him. I have told you he mistreats me terribly. Yesterday, he hurt me again. I know he is supposed to be my husband, but he is not taking care of me. Is there a law to help me be free of him? I fear there is not."

"I do not know." She patted my arm. "If you left him, where would you go?"

"Mother's home would not be the right place for me for long. I want to disappear and officially change my name to only Tabitha. Mother wanted to give me my birth mother's name, Tabitha. I was surprised when Father called me Meydl Tabitha when he introduced me to Jacob's family, but he continued to call me Meydl when we were together."

"How would you travel? How can you be sure he does not follow you and beat you worse for leaving?"

"I am fearful of Uzziah, and I need a plan to take care of myself. I want to look for thread, not easily broken when I sew." I did not know the answers to her questions but vowed to find them.

"Look for thread? Jerusalem is a larger place with many people and shops. You may find work there, or perhaps you could go and beg with others outside the Temple."

"I will not beg."

"I know, but I wanted to at least start with a suggestion for you." Lottie wiped her hands on her tunic and folded them across her ample belly.

"Mother lives with Naomi now, and I do not wish to trouble Phoebe and her new husband. Besides, Uzziah knows the way to their home. I suppose Jerusalem may be a place I could find sewing work, or as a maid in an eating place."

"May I see the herbs now?" Marian said. I had not heard her approach, and I wondered how much she had heard. Perhaps I should tell her everything, but I wanted to protect her.

The three of us walked companionably to a green patch a short way from the house. Parsley, mint, and lemon balm were among the herbs thriving there, and some had dried on the stems.

"I draw water from the well to give them life," said Lottie.

"Will you dry some to hang by your stew kettle?"

"I use them both fresh and dried."

We chatted about medicinal and cooking uses for the herbs. I would have liked to talk longer with Lottie but knew I should go home. I did not want Uzziah to come looking for me and cause trouble for my friends.

"Mother, when can I come home and stay with you?" Marian asked.

I looked at my pretty daughter, with the braided hair caught at the nape of her neck, and realized at the age of twelve she was becoming a woman.

"Your Uncle Uzziah has come home. I would like you to stay with Lottie for now."

"I want to go." Innocent Marian smiled. "Uncle Uzziah may be gone anyway by the time we get there. He usually does not stay long."

Uzziah knew Lottie and Samuel lived a short way down the trail. When we were almost home, I saw him sauntering toward us. I wanted to turn back to Lottie's house when I saw him, but Marian started to run toward him.

He turned, walked toward our house, and went inside. Marian stopped and gazed at me with a perplexed look on her face. We continued on to our home. "Never mind your uncle. He probably did not see you."

When we came into our house, he was seated at the cloth where we eat.

"Meydl," he yelled, "Fetch me some bread, cheese, and wine. I am starved after last night." He raised his eyebrows and grinned lasciviously.

It was too late to place my hands over Marian's eyes or ears, and I frowned at him. My plan had been to go with Marian to see Mother, but with Uzziah home, I wondered if we could. Without a word, I went to the cupboard and brought out fresh barley bread and cheese along with a cup of water for him.

He did not greet Marian, and I was frightened as I saw the unseemly way he gazed at her. He grabbed the bread and broke off a large chunk and stuffed it into his mouth. He cut off a piece of soft cheese and ate it, then licked his fingers. When he picked up the cup of water and took a large gulp, he looked at me and glared. "Where is my wine?"

"There is no wine."

"You do not want me to have wine?" He snarled.

"No."

"We will see!" He rose and began to look around the hut. He went to the shelves and moved the container of flour and sacks of grain. He reached for a flask of oil, sniffed it and dropped it down. Olive oil gurgled and bled a golden pool onto the floor. He began to fling kitchen crockery around and some broke into colorful crumbs. He grabbed the mat on which I had slept and threw it at the wall. He looked at Marian as if she had suddenly appeared, and commanded, "You! Go on to Lottie's house."

Shocked, I gave Marian a contrite look, and whispered, "You know the way. Go quickly and stay there." Fear glistened in her large eyes as she fled. I wanted to go with her, but I knew he would follow and overtake me. I was grateful he had sent her away, as I was afraid of what could happen and what else she would see. I wanted to leave as well but remained out of fear.

When he had torn the place apart, he lunged at me and threw me on the hard, earthen floor amid the broken shards and olive oil. My headscarf flew off and my garments slipped above my knees when I fell. He dropped himself on top of me and began tearing at my clothes.

"Where did you hide the wine?"

"I told you. We have none. Do you think you will find it inside my clothing?" I knew my words incited, but I could not help it.

He slapped my cheek hard and raised his hand to strike again. He grabbed me tightly as one being tied, and I could not escape. I wanted to call to out for help but thought it was useless.

My face burned and became numb as he continued to hit me until my lips and nostrils bled. "Please," I said. But I could say no more as he bit my lip and kissed me forcefully, and I could not breathe.

I had to fight back and clamped his lip between my teeth, but it did not deter him. He was like a demon, ravaging me unmercifully. I had to find a way to get out for I was afraid he would kill me. Blackness overcame me.

In the morning, he was gone. I pleaded with the Lord, doubting he heard me. "Please, what shall I do?" I was determined to leave my hut forever but did not know where to go, and how I would live. Many moon cycles went by, and I felt hopeless. I dreamed of being able to go in search of unbreakable thread but thought it was impossible.

I reminisced about the times when I was a child and my family celebrated our religious holidays. Father had taught me what I knew of our faith. God was the

Creator of everything and he was in control. On lean years, one did not complain but always waited for the good harvest to come in another year. We observed the festive holidays with food, candles, and prayers. He said prayers for meals and thanked the Lord when it rained. I adopted my parent's way of life and assumed men could speak with the Lord.

I went to see Lottie and Marian. It raised my spirits every time I saw my friend and daughter. Before I went home, Lottie and Samuel gave me a flask of wine. "It will help you sleep," he said. I hid it without drinking more than a swallow, as I never knew when Uzziah would come home.

The next morning, when I sat down to milk the nanny goat, no stream of milk went into the bucket. I did not know how old she was as she had belonged to my neighbor, and her kid had been weaned over two years ago and sold. What else could go wrong? Was it a test of my faith as the story father told about Job? I feared it was a sign the Lord had abandoned me or had not been with me.

Twelve

I recovered slowly from Uzziah's rough treatment, and my body began to feel stronger. Yet my inmost pain lingered as silent tears. I could not dwell on my bad marriage to him forever and used sewing to occupy my hands and mind. While I stitched, I day-dreamed of searching for unbreakable thread.

I made and embroidered a yellow tunic and was pleased. Making garments might be a way to earn money, so I could live without accepting charity. While all my fabrics and threads had been lost in the fire, except Marian's basket, neighbors had supplied me with a few things. I skipped with joy as I went to see Lottie and Marian to show them the tunic and share my plan to sew clothing for my livelihood.

"Lottie, I was wondering if you and Samuel are going to Jerusalem any time soon. I want to go there and was hoping we could travel together."

"What a wonderful idea. It is the month of *Tishri*, and *The Festival of Booths* is a few days away. While we have little harvest to bring, I think Samuel wants to go."

"Oh, thank you. We can all be together." I opened my sack and brought out my new tunic. "Do you like it?"

"It is beautiful," Lottie said. "Surely it is for you or Marian."

"It must be for mother." Marian hugged it to herself and smiled.

"I want to wear it to Jerusalem or sell it to make money," I said.

"You could offer your lovely embroidered scarves." Lottie sounded excited for me. She turned toward the kitchen. "Mia, please tell Samuel I have fresh bread for him."

He came from the field, washed his hands in a basin, and beamed a smile at us. "Good day to you, Tabitha." He kissed Lottie on both cheeks and patted Marian on the head. "Lottie, you summoned me for some matter other than bread."

"Yes, we want to know if you want to go to Jerusalem for the Festival."

"Yes, I plan to make the trip. Are we all to go? We have to make preparations."

In the next few days, Samuel concentrated on getting everything ready for us, including a tent pack on his back. During the festival, we three would live in it.

"Are you all packed?" Lottie beamed a smile at me as I came in the early morning we were to leave.

"I am all set." Instead of wearing my new tunic, I folded and packed it and a scarf I had embroidered. I wanted to sell the scarf or trade for good thread and cloth. Into my sack, I tucked a round of bread and tied a flask of water to my belt. It would be two or more days walk by the trail. I was elated.

"We will be on foot, but someday I will be able to buy a donkey." Samuel strode along, using a staff.

Marian hurried after me and handed me a simple, undyed scarf she had woven. "The yarn kept shifting when I tugged hard, but I finished this for you."

"What a beautiful thing you have made. I shall wear it proudly." I pulled off my travel scarf and wrapped hers around my head, smiling. We embraced again.

"Mother, enjoy the trek." Marian and Mia waved.

We carried our belongings and a staff for steadiness on the rocky parts of the trail. My head was full of many thoughts and feelings—adventure and a little fear of not knowing what was ahead. After all, Jacob had been traveling when he was robbed and left for dead.

"Our weather is dry and good for travel," Samuel said. He was a quiet man, and I was surprised when he broke the silence.

"It is a beautiful day and not hot as yet." Lottie walked with me as Samuel led the way. "If you tire, Tabitha, please let us know. We do not have to hurry."

"I am thankful and happy you are both with me."

It was good to have my thoughts diverted, as I did not want to think about fearful happenings.

Samuel was patient with us, but I could see he would have liked to walk faster. Sometimes I worried we would lose sight of him. But he looked behind him from time to time and slowed his pace. There were people on the route, some with donkeys and carts or riding camels, and others on foot. It was a pleasant trip with Lottie's constant patter. "There are no trees nearby save small bushes, so where do you suppose those birds make their nests?" She pointed to a mostly blue sky. "The fluffy cloud looks like a lamb."

I smiled at her observation, enjoyed the pastime. "Look, I think I see a white wolf. The poor lamb will be devoured."

"The lamb has disappeared. I suppose he ate it." We giggled like girls at our silliness. It grew dark, and we walked as far as we could in the cool night and made our beds on a dry grassy area. We rose when it was yet dark to start walking before the sun grew hot and hoped to arrive there by nightfall.

As we approached Jerusalem, I could see the temple. It was like a majestic king of buildings overpowering the landscape in the setting sun. I felt overwhelmed by the throngs of people in the streets of the city. Tents were set up as well as makeshift booths for the festival. People were selling all manner of goods: crockery, jewelry, cloth, yarn, breads, figs, dates, grain, vegetables, olive oil, and wine. My spirits lifted as I could peruse the booths to seek the unbreakable thread I desired.

The noisy din became louder the closer we came to the temple gates. Strange spice aromas mingled with animal dung and human odors tickled my nostrils. Animals being sold for sacrifice were in pens and birds were in dovecotes in the yard. Tables were set up in the courtyard for men to change money from other coinages to the local currency. It was meant to provide a service for people to pay their temple dues.

Beggars sat in the dusty area in front of the stone steps pleading for alms. Some were women with small children curled in their laps. They spoke with their dark eyes. I felt sorry for them and wished I could help the mothers. One aggressive man stepped in front of Samuel and did not let him pass. "Sir, I will starve if you do not give me something to eat." Samuel reached into his pack and brought out a round of bread. He tore off a chunk for the man and offered it. The man scoffed, "Is one morsel all you can give a poor man?" He grabbed the bread, and held his other hand out, expecting money.

"Truly, I am not a rich man." Samuel raised his arm and took a step toward the small man, who retreated, swearing.

"I would not have hit him, but he did not know."

"I want to find someone with whom to trade my embroidered scarf for coins, cloth, or thread." I was fascinated by all the wares for sale and eager to participate.

"Please wait. Let us rest our feet," said Lottie. "Over there I see a spot in the shade we can sit."

"I will, but for a short while." I sat but sneezed as dust curled into my nostrils. Much foot traffic caused it.

"There is a market street with many who trade for goods." Lottie pointed toward a side street leading toward the main one. "There you may look for the precious thread you want." She gave me a knowing smile.

"Yes, I will go and meet you and Samuel here at the temple grounds before long." I stood and grabbed my sack, as I was too excited to sit still and watch others rush past.

"Shall I go with you?" Lottie asked.

"No, I think all will be well with me." I did not want to be a burden.

"I will stay put for now," Lottie said, "but be careful."

"Thieves can be crafty and empty your bag without your knowing. When the shadow is cast upon yonder stone, we will meet here." Samuel said, "I have some trading to do at the market, and we will walk with you, but we may go our own ways once we are there." He had not sat. Lottie frowned and stood to go with him.

"Thank you. I will return," I said.

"Soon we must set up our tent for the night," Lottie said. "Oh, look over there, Tabitha, so many colorful garments." Her eyes shone.

We shopped awhile before we went to our beds in the tent. I hardly slept as I anticipated selling my tunic and searching for thread. The next morning, Lottie and I walked to the clothing booth area.

"Clothing in many colors I have not ever seen." I wanted to take it all in. It was not long before I had lost sight of Lottie. I watched a woman who was using a spindle to spin threads from wool. Balls of plain yarn were heaped in a basket beside her. I wished I had coins to buy thread, but all I had were a couple of small coins and the beautiful embroidered scarf I wanted to sell. "You seem to be an expert with the spindle. I spin thread much slower as I have no tool like yours," I said. "Do you make unbreakable thread?"

The woman spoke to me in a strange language and continued to spin fibers into thread she wrapped into a ball. She spun strands of thread similar to the ones I used and some broke as she wound them around. I walked on.

A thin man in a ragged tunic watched me as I strolled among the vendors. He eyed my bag. As I mingled with the crowd, he edged his way until he was beside me. I watched him bump into the person standing next to me. During the sudden scuffle and apologies, he kept glancing at me. I felt uneasy as I lingered by booths of jewelry and crockery. Keeping at a distance among people, I thought he continued to observe me as I touched scarves in another booth. While I spoke with the woman there, admiring her wares, I did not reach inside my garment for money as I did not have enough to buy anything.

A plump, olive-skinned woman spoke to me in Aramaic. "You like my scarves, why do you not try one on to see how it feels. The yellow and red with the green embroidery would suit you well."

"I sew things," I said, and reached into my sack to bring out the lavishly embroidered tunic for the woman to see. It was a decision I made without thinking it through.

"Ahh, you do beautiful work. I know someone who would pay a good price for it. You and I could work together." Her small thick hands eagerly reached up to touch it.

"Who would buy? Please show me as I need to meet my friends soon." I looked at the length of the shadows of people and decided it was time to go to the place Samuel and Lottie said they would meet me.

"The customer I have in mind is not here. If you would like to leave the garment with me, I can make sure she gets it and pays for it. I will keep part of the money for my work, of course."

"I do not know when I will return here." I was tempted to trust the woman, but I might never see her again. "Pay me for the garment, and then you can sell it to the woman you have in mind and get your money back."

"I do not have enough money, but I will give you the lovely scarf you admired as surety." She looked away toward the man standing at a nearby booth, the one I had seen earlier looking at me. "Gestas," she hissed, pointing out the man with a mop of matted brown hair and unkempt beard.

"What?" I asked and saw the wiry man slink away into the crowd.

"Nothing. A man I do not like. He is a cheat and a thief. Be careful around him." She spat the words out in a hiss. She stood holding the scarf for me to try on, and when I did, she said, "You look beautiful in it. It is perfect for you."

I hesitated, trying to decide what to do because I did not need a scarf. I made all my own garments. "The scarf will not be enough. Can you also give me some money?"

"Will this do?" The woman held out her plump hand in which she had four small coins. "It is all I can spare."

"Two more, and I will wait for the rest of the money and collect it when I return." I did not know when I would return and wondered if I was foolish to make the trade.

"It is done." She drew out two *mites*. She stood, lifted the tunic and pressed the bodice to her bosom to see how it would look. "I like it."

I felt sad as I turned away with the new scarf wrapped smartly around my head. I put Marian's into my pack. Any garments I had made had been for family or close friends, and I would see them again. I did not know when or if I would be able to come here, but I decided to trust her. Had I made a mistake to do so?

As I hurried toward Lottie and Samuel's meeting place, Gestas stepped out of the shadow of a building and bumped into me. He looked at me with piercing ebony eyes. The six coins I had were loose inside my bag with my scarves. "Sorry," I said, and moved aside, remembering what the woman had warned. When I did, he stepped the same direction and grinned toothless at me, shaking his head. He brushed against me and was gone.

When I reached inside the bag only my scarves and two small coins remained. I wanted to scream but did not want to attract attention. I went back to the spot where we had run into each other, thinking the money had fallen to the ground, but it was not there. The man was nowhere in sight, and although I did not know how he had done it, I was sure he had stolen my coins. I was disappointed beyond words, disheartened, and wanted to cry.

I met Lottie and Samuel as planned and did not tell them of the incident with the thief. Samuel had warned me, so I did not want to let him know it had happened.

"What a beautiful scarf," Lottie said.

"I traded it for the tunic I brought, and received some money too."

"You did well," Samuel said. "I have paid my temple dues and am ready to go home soon. Lottie is tired."

"We can leave if you want." I had thought we would be staying another day. It meant I had made the trade for my tunic and did not know if I would be able to claim the balance of what the woman owed. I wanted to return to the market street to plead with the woman to return my tunic, but I did not want to ask my friends to delay. We slept outside of town and began our trek home before daybreak.

After one and a half days travel, the sun was heading on its way to the horizon when we neared my hut. I longed to go inside and lay on my mat. "Please tell Marian I will see her in the morning, and we will talk all day. Thank you both again for everything you are doing for me, and especially going with me to Jerusalem. I had a wonderful time. Have a good evening."

"You have a good rest, and we will see you tomorrow. I enjoyed the trip with you." Lottie said.

I felt elated at the experience of seeing the holy city of Jerusalem and the markets. It gave me hope. There was more to life than my lost farm. Lottie and I kissed cheeks, and I turned toward my house.

I stopped when I looked up at my home. I felt downcast. Uzziah, his face thin and gaunt, squatted by the door. Without standing to greet me, he squinted, and snarled, "Where have you been?"

Thirteen

ot anger crept to my face. "It is a fine question since you have been away much longer. I went to Jerusalem for the Festival of Booths with Lottie and Samuel."

"Did you bring any wine?"

"No, but I got this scarf. Is it not beautiful?"

"You had money to buy something for yourself but nothing for your husband." Uzziah gestured wildly with his hand as if to swat away a flying bug.

"I did not know you were coming home." I raised my voice, decided not to say more. Without wine to embolden him, maybe he would be kind. "It was refreshing for me to travel." When he was silent, I asked, "How have you been?"

"You do not want to know. I have been hiding from the Romans. They are seizing every able man for their army. Someone told me they are not taking devout Jews, but I do not believe it. I have joined the Zealots who want to overthrow the Romans so we can go back to our way of life without their interference and taxation. They are arresting any of us they find. I kept away from strong drink and starved, eating discarded food I found and drinking little water. Do you see how thin I am?"

"Yes, I have eyes. I am going inside now." I was too tired to do anything, and I was hungry. "Barley bread will be ready in due time if you want to eat."

Candles flickered, casting eerie shadows in the small hut. We supped in silence and I was grateful he did not continue to berate me or anyone. He did not mention wine. I thought he might have given it up when he joined the Zealots, and I was thankful. I kept hidden the flask Samuel and Lottie had given me. I did have many questions concerning where Uzziah had been for two years and, more importantly, why he had come home. He probably had no place to go.

"With your father gone, why did you not go to your mother to live instead of this hut? She's on the farther side of Samuel's place." Grieved, I flinched at his words as if he had struck me, rose from the mat, and cleared the dishes. I feared anything I said would provoke his anger.

He stood, and his yellowed eyes, glowing from the candle gleam, surveyed the shelf on which I kept flour and grains. He strode and peered inside the bin. He growled and dumped its meager contents on the floor, creating a powdery white dust. He moved a grain sack, an empty crock, and looked behind them. He found the wine flask Samuel and Lottie had given to me. "You meant to keep this from me." He raised his hand toward my face, and I glared at him, reaching for a long-handled ladle. He lowered his hand, shook his finger at me, grabbed the flask and stormed outside.

I feared he would be drunk and mean when he came inside. My only choice was to leave the house, so I put on my cloak, took my travel staff and walked out. It was preferable to being trapped inside. He was in the darkness somewhere, and I meant to avoid him. My eyes adjusted to the blackness around me, and I looked up to a moonless void. There were few stars, and a haze of clouds dimmed them. I walked slowly, steadily, on the cool trail toward Lottie's house. My staff was a ready defense. I listened and at first, heard the call of a night bird. My feet made a light noise in the dirt.

I heard him slurping the wine and belching. He would drink until it was empty. Suddenly he was behind me and grabbed one shoulder. I swung around with the staff in hand and startled him, knocking him down. I began to run.

He caught me, wrestled the staff from my hands. As he pushed me to the ground, I landed on a thorny bush. Blood trickled down my scratched face, and my hands smarted. My staff lay nearby. I sprang up, screamed as loudly as I could, and hoped Samuel and Lottie would hear. Uzziah slapped at me, and though he missed more than hit, I grew angrier and found increased courage with each swing of his hand.

"You should not have let the house burn and the land go to tax collectors." While he stumbled about ranting at me, he managed to stay on his feet and kept punching the air.

I recovered my staff, crouched, and swung it at him. He ducked, but not enough. A sickening crack sounded as the staff connected with his head, and he fell to the hard-packed earth with a thud. I had stubbed my foot on a large stone and wondered if he had fallen on it.

It was deathly quiet. I was relieved, shocked, and frightened all at once. My whole being was involved in a moment I had no control over. I screamed. I felt drained, as if my life was fading away.

Samuel came carrying an oil torch. "Tabitha, are you injured? We heard you cry out."

Weak-kneed, I sank down, distraught and dazed. "I am a little hurt, but Uzziah may need help. Can you see if he is all right? He must have hit his head on a stone when I knocked him to the earth with my staff," I said, and stood with wobbly legs.

"I will see," Samuel put a protective arm around my shoulder. "You are bleeding so we will get you inside and clean your wounds." When I nodded, he held onto my arm until we got to my hut as it was nearer than their place. Satisfied I was safe, he went to Uzziah.

I cleaned the grime and blood from my face and hands where the briars had scraped and scratched. I dabbed halfheartedly with a wet rag at stains on my tunic. My life pulse drummed in my ears.

After a while, Samuel returned. In the lamplight, I could tell by the grave expression on his face something was wrong. "I believe he is dead, as I can feel no breath coming from him." His voice was unemotional.

"No, no, I did not mean to kill him," I cried out. The shock of it set my head spinning, and I thought I would fall. I doubled over, my hands covered my eyes.

"He is thin, and I believe he was about to die from some other cause. He hastened his end fighting you." Samuel touched my shoulder, consoling.

I cried uncontrollable tears. There had been many times I had wished him dead, now he was, no doubt by my hands. I feared I would be stoned for killing him.

Samuel went to get another servant, Sheaf, to help with Uzziah's body. We would have prepared his body and buried him in the cave with Jacob and his father, but when they came to the place Samuel had left him, he was gone. The men shouted his name over and over. Samuel called, "Uzziah, if you are alive, please let me know your whereabouts so we can bind your wounds."

There was no answer, and the night was dark with a sliver of moon and clouds dimming the stars. He and Sheaf, along with other servants, continued to call and look for Uzziah in the dark, but he had vanished. In the morning Samuel and Sheaf looked for any sign of him. There were paw prints on the trail and signs of dragging, yet no blood. They were stopped at a thicket. Upon examination of the brush, no sign of him was found. Uzziah had disappeared.

Fourteen

As he awakened, Uzziah became aware of the damp, musty air, and the cold stone floor on which he lay. "Oh, my head, my head," he groaned, wretched, shattered, as never before. When he tried to move his right arm, it was painful so he used the other to reach across himself. Blood and dried grit stuck to his torn ragged right sleeve. "What happened to me last night?" He had been drunk many evenings, and a few times awakened in strange places with various bruises from a fight, but nothing like this. "Where am I, in a cavern?" There was no one to listen, at least he presumed not. Had someone thrown him in a cave for his grave? How had he gotten here?

The hair on his arm prickled upright as he heard a mewling and snuffling somewhere below. If there were baby animals, a mother could appear any moment and have him for their sup. He needed to get out, rolled over in pain and scooted on his belly, gained a foothold and crawled toward what he hoped was the entrance. Cool air moved across him, and though he saw deep darkness, he glimpsed freedom. Painful and confined, he could not move fast, but kept going. The way became narrower, but a gleam of light ahead energized him toward it. He felt faint and thirsty but determined to keep moving out. Full light blinded him until he blinked several times as he came to the mouth of the cave.

Free of the confines of it, he rolled down an incline and landed in a thicket where he became scratched and scraped. Had a she lion had found him and taken him to her den? He lay there among thorns, thinking, hoping the lioness would not return and drag him back inside. He sucked in great breaths of air. Slowly and painfully he remembered the quarrel with his wife and how she had come at him with a staff. She had knocked him out and left him to die. Meanwhile, the lioness must have grabbed his arm between her teeth, took him as easy prey to her family. Confused, he did not know which direction would be the way home and thought it best not to go there. She wanted him dead, and he was weak and unable to defend himself. Voices in the distance echoed, and he was sure his ears were ringing with deceptive noises. No one would call to him.

With great effort, he stood on shaky legs. In the pale morning light, he could see there was a valley below. There were a few small trees, mostly brush, and hope of finding a fallen branch to use as a staff faded away.

Walk or run, he thought. He no longer spoke out loud to himself like a madman. He wanted to know where the lioness was, and if she could pick up his scent.

He tried to remember his father's words of wisdom and wished he had listened more carefully to his instruction. "If you are pursued by man or beast, seek the direction of the wind and do not let your scent drift toward those who would harm you." He wanted his father to be beside him for protection. Father had always welcomed him home and tried to help him grow into the man he wanted him to be. He did not want to be like his father, toiling from dawn until dusk. Jacob was the same. He could not understand how they got any pleasure out of life.

There had been a couple of times Uzziah had been this afraid. Once he had been thrown into jail falsely accused of murder. A friend of his father knew the judge, and the case was dismissed when the real culprit was caught. Another time, after many days of enjoyment, drinking with friends and buying pleasure with prostitutes, he was penniless. He was sleeping among the beggars, sitting, holding out his hands in the streets when his father's friend grabbed him and got him to stand. "You should be ashamed, Uzziah. Get yourself up on my cart." He drove him home.

He laughed, tears rolled down his cheeks, and he was parched. Despite the chafing of the stones and thorns beneath his feet, he bade them keep moving. He saw a nest tucked in a bush. Perhaps he could find an egg and suck the contents. He reached in, scraped his hand on twigs, only to find a furry chick, and cursed. He did not know when the mother bird would return and did not want to find out.

His legs were like dry unbending stalks as he put one foot in front of the other. No sandals protected him and his soles chafed. "Meydl," he said her name quietly, "Tabitha," but spit it out in disgust. When his brother was married to her, he thought she was the most beautiful, unattainable woman in all the earth and wanted her above any woman he had known. Yet, when Jacob died and he became her husband by law, he found her to be cold and unyielding. She hated everything he did and let him know it. He wondered how he could have ever wanted such a one as her. He had no home, no property, and it was her doing. The lands were lost to taxes, and the biggest insult was his father's house was burned and gone.

His mind was lost in delirium as he hobbled along. He thought he heard singing in the distance, and the sound of cartwheels and clomping hooves. He shook his head to clear his ears and still heard them drawing nigh. He saw dust being kicked up, so walked toward the sounds. A carriage drawn by two donkeys came closer. He waved his arms in hopes they would see him and stop. Yet they might think he was a thief. He cleared his throat. With all his strength he called, "Hail to you this fine morning."

Twittering laughter came from behind colorful

curtains. The dark-skinned man at the reins waved but did not speak. Foreign traveling bands had the reputation of robbing people. Uzziah had nothing, so thought there was no danger. "May I walk along with you?" The man threw up his hands and spoke in his language to the lighter colored man who sat with him up front. The carriage slowed. The men traded places without stopping, a wonder to behold.

"My name is Wills. The man you spoke to, Horatio, does not understand Aramaic. Are you in need of help? You look as if you have been through a fight."

"I am Uzziah. Yes, a fight, and I woke up in a cave above a brushy hill. I do not know how I got there."

"Ah, I have also awakened in strange places after a wild night. It happens if a man lives a full life." His dark eyes sized him like a man looking at his barley field, and said, "You need a drink?' He handed him the flask without waiting for an answer.

Uzziah tipped it to his lips and found it was fresh spring water. It tasted like the best liquor as he quenched his thirst. "Thank you."

"Keep it, I have more. Want to walk with us?" They had slowed to a stop.

'Yes, where are you going?"

"Wherever our carriage takes us on this trail. I thought you might be local and tell us how far to the nearest town."

"Alas, I am lost and this trail is unfamiliar."

Laughter came from inside and women began to

sing as they moved. With renewed energy from the water, he had strength to walk along. They slowed the donkey so he could keep up. The rising sun indicated they were heading east.

Uzziah became absorbed in thought. He always wanted to have everything Jacob had. His mother loved and doted on him, but his father was devoted to Jacob. He ordered Uzziah to come to the fields and work. He gave him the most menial tasks to do. His hands bled from handling dry stalks, and his back pained him from reaping a grain field. He murmured, "He never gave me a chance."

Thoughts about his life and his befuddled head kept his mind occupied so he failed to notice surroundings. He glanced at the carriage and saw a young face with dark eyes and brown curls peering from behind a yellow curtain. The voice piped, "Who are you?"

"I am Uzziah, and who are you?"

"Silas."

Wills had jumped down beside them and spoke to the boy. Silas smiled, waved, and ducked behind the curtain.

"I told my son to stop bothering you. You have much on your mind."

"It was all right. I was surprised he spoke in Aramaic."

"My boy's language ability is good. We will tell you tales by the campfire some evening."

"Thank you, Wills. My head is feeling faint and my

legs do not want to move anymore. I appreciate coming with you, but I must find a place to rest."

"Do you see the spot of green off in the distance? My wife has been begging me to stop so we will rest when we get there if you can last."

"I will try." Sore feet stepped onward. When he had heard Wills say, "by the campfire some evening," he was hopeful they would let him continue traveling with them.

The cart came to a stop by a grove of old olive trees and other small trees. There was a spring of water flowing. Children and women scrambled from the cart and ran toward the cover of brush to one side. Wills, Horatio, and Silas walked toward another taller thicket on the opposite side. Uzziah followed them.

Soon they were all sitting on a grassy slope, listening to the sound of the cool waters gently flowing over rounded rocks. Baskets of dried fruits, loaves of bread, and a cooking pot were brought out. The men built a fire and set up a contraption so a vessel of stew could be suspended above the flames. Children begged for dates, figs, and other fruit, and their mothers put one in each child's hand, nodded toward the large kettle of stew, and spoke to them.

An elderly white-bearded man had stayed inside until food was served. Wills and Silas helped him down. "This is my father, Elias," Wills said. Everyone showed the elder respect as he ambled about with the aid of a staff. They found some fallen branches. Horatio assembled the meager wood and placed pieces together to form a low seat for Elias.

"Thank you, I cannot get down on the ground and back up by myself." Elias eased himself onto the rug covered makeshift chair.

Uzziah reclined, half interested in food, but Wills invited him to partake when the family ate. "Come, my wife makes wonderful tasting vegetable stew."

After he had satisfied his appetite, an olive tree provided shade and there was soft grass beneath it. He wanted to sleep but could not. Silas bent next to his ear and said, "Did you know there was once a king named Uzziah?"

"No, I had not heard."

"It was a very long time ago. He was a bad king. Why did your father give you such a name?"

"Silas, come here!" Wills called, and his son obeyed.

Uzziah did not think much about the bad king who had the same name. He had watched with interest as Wills, his family, and his servants with children all supped together. The stew and bread brought some energy to his bones. He had nothing to lose traveling with these people and was lulled to sleep.

Loud shrieking filled the air and he woke with a start. The travelers were in motion and the women screaming. He saw a band of mean-looking men had invaded the camp, brandishing swords. Women hurried the children and themselves into the cart, but the men were standing their ground until all were inside. Elias was lifted into the cart. Although Uzziah was not in any condition to fight, he stood by Silas and Horatio, ready. The stew pot had been kicked over and the fire flickered to ashes.

"We have no gold or precious stones, nothing of value for you to steal," Wills said. Two men menaced with swords and answered in a foreign language. Wills retorted in their tongue.

The servant who had been at the reins slapped the donkeys into action, and sped away, leaving Wills, Silas, Horatio, and Uzziah. They were saving the women and children.

Uzziah was suddenly grabbed from behind and thrown to the ground. The man grabbed and tore off his outer cloak, and ran his hands over his shirt and tunic. He uttered some profane words. A searing pain lashed Uzziah's chest as a heavy boot stomped on it. He tried to tuck his hand beneath his torn tunic. His last feeling was the pain of his father's gold ring being ripped off. Blackness overcame him.

Fifteen

After my apparent murder of Uzziah, my heart filled with mixed emotions of guilt, fear, regret, and relief. Lottie came and tried to get me to eat something, but I refused with a side-to-side head shake. I could not speak at first.

"You must take care of yourself." Lottie offered a cup of mint tea. She shook my arm slightly as if to rouse me from sleep.

"What will happen to me? Can I be stoned to death for slaying him? What about Marian?" I could think of nothing else. All the grief I had for Jacob weighed like a heavy rock inside me. To mourn his brother was as impossible as a chore one dreads. The tea I sipped helped soothe my anxious thoughts. "Thank you, Lottie, for coming here."

"No one knows what happened to Uzziah. Samuel told me he most likely died from many years of strong drink. Some day we may find his bones and clothing ravaged by a lion or other wild beast. Anyone who knew you would not believe you killed him." Lottie held me. "He could not walk away, and I do not expect he will return."

"I do not know what to hope. I need to go to Jerusalem to give a temple offering." I had a strong desire to ask for forgiveness and to give thanks to the Lord my life had been spared.

"There is no need for you to atone. You have little enough as it is, but if you insist, we will go to Jerusalem with you."

"I cannot stay any longer, because the memory of killing Uzziah keeps me wakeful. I want to go far away as I have wanted to do for some time to look for unbreakable thread. Only sweet Marian keeps me here." I wept.

"Lie down and get some rest. Maybe in a few days, your thoughts will settle. I will ask Samuel when we can accompany you to Jerusalem. Marian can stay with Mia. Soon travel will not be easy as winter will be upon us. I think you should not go at all."

"Do not trouble Samuel. I know the way you showed me, so I can go."

"It is too dangerous for you to travel alone." Lottie shook her head.

Deep guilt plagued me. I had little to offer to the Lord at the temple treasury but thought I must. Despite the fact I had loathed Uzziah, I felt conflicted about killing him. I wanted him dead, and I had committed a grievous sin. If he was deceased as Samuel thought, and a wild animal had taken his body away, I still held myself responsible. He had not been buried as he should have been with his father and brother.

Samuel and Lottie traveled with me to Jerusalem, walking. I went to the market street to look for the woman to whom I had traded the beautiful tunic for a scarf during the Festival of Booths. The city did not excite me as it had the first time I saw it. There were many wares for sale, but the woman who got my tunic was not among the sellers. I turned away in despair. I had no food save for a bit of flour at home to bake bread. I lost sight of Lottie and Samuel, and they had not said where they would meet me. I had told them many times I wanted to go away to start a new life and look for unbreakable thread. I asked the Lord if my life was over. Did he listen? Prayer was useless as he dwelled in the distant blue skies. Tears welled up, but I bade them not to fall.

I grasped my last two tiny coins. I looked at my small hands and wondered how they were capable of causing another human to die. I thrust them inside the folds of my wheat-colored tunic. What could I do with the two coins? I might buy a handful of meal to bake a meager round of bread. It would satisfy the gnawing ache in my stomach. Since I had no other food, I would eventually become weak and lie down and die anyway. Would the money make any difference? When I was a child, Father said everything belonged to the Lord.

As I approached the temple, I thought of how it would be to sit in the dust among the beggars and plead for alms. I thrust my chin up, and squared my shoulders, for my pride prevented such a thing. People approached the temple and dropped gifts into the treasury box. The Pharisees, dressed in fine robes, made a great show of putting in gold and silver coins. I wondered if their garments were made with unbreakable thread. My cloak was frayed and mended many times. I held back and waited until the surrounding crowd was occupied in conversation.

Timidly, I tiptoed up to the treasury box and pulled my right hand from the folds of my clothing. My fist held tightly to the coins. I was reluctant to show the little I had to give, but I opened my hand. Perspiration on my palms made the coppers stick to my skin, preventing them from dropping at first. I looked up quickly to see if anyone had noticed. The small coins left my palm, one at a time, and fell into the box without a sound. I had done it. I bowed my head, looked to the stone floor and hoped no one had noticed. It was done, even if I thought the Lord might not see.

When I looked up, I saw a bearded young rabbi teaching some men to my left. He had dark uncut hair of a man from Nazareth. His kind brown eyes were directed toward me as he spoke to his followers, who turned to look at me. I was embarrassed as I thought he pitied me and might be talking about me. I slipped into the midst of a group of people who stood nearby and walked with them for a time until I was clear of the temple steps.

"Tabitha, over here," Lottie called and came to me. "Did you see the woman to whom you sold the tunic?"

"No." I shook my head and looked away. I did not want to cry and mostly did not want my friend to see. "I gave my last coins to the Lord."

Lottie shook her head, paused, said, "I am sorry about your lost tunic. Samuel is doing business with the moneychangers. He was arguing they had cheated him, and would not leave until they corrected their mistake. It may take a while." She rolled her eyes. "Let us find a booth with something to eat."

"You may, but I am not hungry."

"Come." Lottie grabbed my hand as we walked among the throngs of people. She stopped by a man who was selling fresh and dried fruits. "May I taste your figs before I buy?"

The man cut the fruit and handed us a sample of fresh figs and sweet dates, which we both ate. "I would like some of those figs," said Lottie, and held out a coin.

The man took a knife and started to cut a large fig in two. She handed him two more coins. He gave her three figs and held up the dates. "These are the most delicious and cheapest price you will find anywhere."

Lottie brought out two coins and he added dates to her carry bag. My hunger was satisfied after eating the delicious fruit.

"Stay near here and I will see if Samuel is ready."

One of the young men who had been with the teacher came near. His eyes were a lighter brown than most people I knew. He was barefoot and wore a tan tunic and no cloak. I was taken with the youth's appearance and stared at him. He looked at me and nodded but did not speak. As he walked away, I thought perhaps he was going to be with his teacher. I was drawn to follow him but kept at a discreet distance, pausing now and then to look at thread spinners and fabric. I scolded myself for not staying where Lottie could find me.

The young man stopped and turned to me. "Woman, you have given much."

"Do you mock me? You watched when I offered my little coins."

"Not mocking at all. Jesus told us you gave more than everyone, all you had to live on." His voice was strong, yet pleasant like one singing.

"How did he know?" I whispered. Feeling my face warm with redness, I wanted to get away.

"He is the Lord's son. Blessed are you," he said and slipped into the crowd.

"The Lord's son?" Awestricken, I could not wait to tell Lottie who would never believe what I had heard.

I went to find her and perused booths along the way to look closely at thread spinners. I was surprised to see a familiar figure in the crowd and smiled in spite of the gloom I was feeling.

Zeke the Rug Man led a donkey with bells on its neck. They wove in and out among the crowd, and people stopped to admire his colorful rugs. When he saw me, his face shone with a smile. "I can't believe my good fortune. How is it we meet in Jerusalem after all this time, eh?" He gave a slight bow, and gray hair dangled beneath his faded red turban.

"I am pleased to see you." I smiled at him.

"What brings you here? You have wares to sell, eh?"

"My scarves. I should have brought my nanny goat."

"The old one you had tethered? I don't know anyone who wants a dried-up old nanny goat, eh." Zeke chuckled.

"Zeke." I laughed, something I had not done for a long time.

"Actually, I know a man who lives in Joppa who might take her. He is a tanner and would buy the hide."

I shook my head at the remark but smiled at the thought. "I have never seen a tanner. I have heard of the Joppa seaport, and I know nothing about the location, yet I do want to go somewhere else as I have no food left in my hut."

"Nothing, eh?" Zeke scratched his head beneath his turban with a forefinger. "I have traveled to Joppa myself and could take you anywhere you wish to go, eh."

"I have not been farther from my hut than the trail to Jerusalem." I looked up at Zeke. "Now I cannot travel as I have no money or food."

"What will ye do, eh?" A frown creased his brow.

"I will not beg. I have nothing, and I intend to return

home to Marian with my friends Samuel and Lottie." I had tears at the thought of leaving my daughter.

Zeke stood absently stroking his donkey's shoulder. He gazed away, looked toward distant hills as if deep in thought. "Would you like to accompany an old man, eh?"

"I should not," I said, but realized it would be an opportunity to get away, and to keep looking for unbreakable thread. People who had been admiring his wares walked on.

"Why not? Who are you beholden to, eh? You can't need to be home for a goat that doesn't give milk."

"Remember, I have a daughter. I must speak to my friends who traveled with me. They take care of my Marian." When I looked beyond Zeke on the roadway, I saw them. "There they are." I waved. "Lottie, here I am."

Lottie and Samuel, their garments rustling, came to me.

"Who is this rug-selling man with you? Is something wrong?" Lottie's red cloak draped over the expanse of her body and swished about her ankles as I motioned to them.

"I am Samuel, and this is my wife Lottie." He came close, frowned, not approving of my speaking with the man.

"Zeke the Rug Man." Zeke extended both hands, palms up.

"You are the one who saved Jacob?" Samuel's frown

disappeared as he recognized Zeke.

"The same, eh." Zeke's hands settled at his sides.

"It is such a pleasure to see you," Lottie gushed. "She needs a good friend like you."

I shook my head and frowned at her, but there was no use trying to stop her.

"I have asked Meydl Tabitha to accompany me on my travels and cook food for me. She thinks she cannot go, eh, because of a nanny goat needs tending."

"I did not . . ." The scorching sun ducked behind a puffy white cloud.

"We can take care of the goat, and we already care for her daughter. I can explain everything to Marian." Lottie's voice had the ring of authority.

"My mind is set against it, as I am concerned for Tabitha. Are you not fearful of the dangers of distant travel?" Samuel's brow creased as he spoke.

"She will do well." Lottie touched my arm.

I could not believe what was happening. I had thought I would trek home and one day die of starvation. A peaceful feeling came over me, and I was as one who is mute, but finally found my tongue. "Yes, Zeke is a kind man, and all will be well. I want to go somewhere to find a new life."

Samuel frowned, opened his mouth to speak, but said nothing.

"I do not want to leave Marian. I must give her to you now, but I will come to see her when I return." Tears formed in my eyes, but they did not spill. If one asked why I was going away with a kind man I knew little about, I could not explain.

"We will love her as our own daughter. We are bound by law to take care of widows and orphans," Samuel said. "We do not expect any payment from you. As to this sudden departure, I do not approve of your traveling alone with a man." His brow creased when he looked at me like a concerned father. "It is dangerous. Are you sure you wish to go?" The sun crept out from behind the cloud, but the air had cooled.

I looked at my friends and paused. "Yes." I sounded hollow, and in my inmost being, I wondered if I had taken leave of my senses. "Please take care of Marian. Tell her I love her and will be home soon."

"Surely." Samuel shook his head. "And now, the day is far spent. I want to rest and start toward home before daybreak. Take good care of her." He clasped arms as a sign of friendship to Zeke. Samuel kissed me on both cheeks. "Turn back if you want. You have a home with us." He showed genuine concern as he looked at me and said, "Go with the Almighty Lord."

"I will treat her well, as I would a sister. She will be a good travel companion, and I look forward to her company."

"Have a safe journey. Do not stay away long." Lottie and I kissed cheeks. We clung to each other and had tears in our eyes as we parted.

I was stunned into silence by Zeke's offer, one I had not suggested. Feeling sure God did not hear my pleas for his help, I had resigned myself to go home and die without ever finding the unbroken thread. Warm sunset would give way to a cool night, and I stood looking at Zeke and his donkey trying to make sense of my situation. True, this was what I thought I had wanted, to go away and start over. I could not believe it was happening but decided to trust. "Thank you, Lord, whose name I cannot say," I uttered, but doubted he listened.

We camped for the night, lying on separate mats beneath some bushes off the side of the trail. The donkey was tethered to a larger stump beside us. Sleep would not come, and I listened to night birds as I finally drifted off.

It was dark in the morning when we ate bread and dried fruits, then rolled up our mats to put on the donkey before we set out on the trail. Zeke was quiet, and I was absorbed in conflicting thoughts about the way chosen for me. Indeed, I did not feel I had much to do with the decision I made.

"Have you found unbreakable thread?" His voice was low but startled me.

"No, I have not. Are we to go on a quest for it?" I kept my voice light and in good humor. The air was still, cool, and comfortable as the sun was making its glorious appearance on the blue horizon.

"Eh? Yes, the thread and so much more," Zeke said, with a twinkle in his eye. We walked beside his laden donkey and carried on an amiable conversation about the weather and sights we had seen in Jerusalem. I enjoyed the walk with his easy companionship, and I was calm as the days wore on.

"We will be in Joppa tomorrow," he said. Sleep came without hesitation as I was exhausted from the trek, and I trusted Zeke to watch out for my safety. When I awakened at predawn, I had a sickening panic as I did not see him or his donkey. Oh, no, he would not have left me alone.

Sixteen

When I stood, I saw the donkey and Zeke coming toward me. They had gone for water and returned. Although I thought about it, I did not thank the Lord, as I was unsure of his hand in my life.

"Are you ready to travel?" Zeke offered me a full flask of fresh water.

Intrigued by the new adventure, I felt hopeful my life was meant to continue. Zeke knew trails and alternate routes, and which ones were prone to dangerous footing or attack by robbers. The air was cooler now. We traveled in a northwest direction from Jerusalem, stopped at Lydda, and went to the walled port city of Joppa to obtain items for the journey. We approached the seaport by the Great Sea.

In Joppa, the atmosphere was brisk and filled with the odors of the sea's bounty. It was a busy place with fishermen and tradesmen who dealt loudly with each other, and people who bartered items for sale. Zeke bought fish from a fisherman who brought in a large catch and bargained with a street vendor for rounds of flatbread to eat with the fish. My stomach gnawed with hunger pangs, and we built a fire on the beach to cook. I thought it was the best tasting fish I ever had.

"The fish tastes wonderful, and I am well fed. Where will we go next?" A breeze lifted the plain cloth we had laid as I gathered up the remains of our meal.

"We are going to Simon's house outside of town near the wall, by the sea. It stinks, eh, because of the animal skins and the process he uses to turn them into leather."

Simon the Tanner was working when we neared. Hides were strung on lines and posts, and stacks of hairy dirty-looking skins waited to be turned into leather. A vat of saltwater held pelts. A musky aroma and the odor of urine filled the air. He was scraping hair from an ox hide. He mopped his brow with the back of his hand as he saw us. "A blessed day to you, Zeke, good to see you again. Who is this fine woman?"

"Meydl Tabitha's a widow, and like a sister to me. I have brought her on my travels to be my cook."

"That is good. Take her to the house to meet Elena. I will be there when I have finished with this hide."

"I would like to look at your fine leathers as I need to buy some." Zeke and I turned toward a house on a sandy rise, not more than a good stone flinger's toss away. A cool gust of wind tugged at my scarf and hair.

"I have choice leather to show you later." Simon bent over the hide again.

It was a roomy home with steps going up to the roof. Thankfully, sea breezes carried the stench of his work away from his abode, but the smell was inescapable. His plump, pleasant wife met us as we came on the path to her front door. "Zeke," she said and smiled at me.

"Elena, meet Meydl Tabitha," he said and kissed Elena's olive-skin cheeks. He talked with her in a language I did not know. After she had spoken, Zeke said, "She offered bread and wine and invited us to spend the night. She speaks *Koine*."

"I have not heard of Koine."

"It is the common Greek tongue," he said.

Elena communicated with me by pointing to things, smiling, and shaking her head. I declined the cheese and bread, but I could not deny my hunger for something that smelled delicious cooking in the kettle.

"Hello to all. I have washed and hope the odors do not offend anyone." Simon stepped inside and greeted his wife with a warm embrace. He poured wine. We all supped a savory fish stew and fresh bread.

"Please stay here. There is a sleeping mat you may use. Put it wherever you are comfortable." Simon pointed to the rolled mat.

"Thank you," I said. After visiting, I curled up on the mat on the floor near the hearth. Zeke tied his donkey by the entrance and slept on the roof. I had first thought I wanted to be in Joppa, but I was reluctant to stay with Simon and Elena because of the tanning odor.

At first light, Elena awakened and went outside to put bread into the oven to bake. I got up, followed her, and asked, by use of hand motions as if drinking from a cup, if there was a well nearby. I wanted to get a drink of water and freshen myself. She handed me a flask and pointed to a path on the far side of her house, and when I was going, Zeke caught up with me.

"Are you ready to travel with me, eh, or do you want to stay here?" He smiled.

"I would like to go away from this place." I wrinkled my nose and pinched it with my fingers.

"One could get used to the smell here, eh, but I was hoping you would journey along with me to some other places I would like to show you."

"I want to go with you." I drew a bucket of water from the well and took a cup from my pack to dip some water to drink. I made a face and sputtered. "It tastes a little salty." I filled Elena's flask.

"It is beside the sea, eh."

On our way to the house, we stopped to watch Simon scrape hides. He was kneeling on a big flat rock on which he had laid an animal skin with hair. In his hand was a scraper made from a large seashell. Nearby was a vat of water in which skins were soaking. Simon stood when he saw us. "I trust you slept well. I hope the smell does not drive you away. Elena and I like your company."

"It does stink, but I am alright." I smiled.

"Much of the odor comes from the dung and urine trough over there where I have to soak and knead the skin to soften it." He held up the hide and dropped it in the foul-smelling liquid. Two small boys came up the trail with outstretched hands. Simon said, "You boys tie your tunics, dance in the trough, and I will pay you."

They bared their brown bodies except for cloth tied between their legs and fastened with a tie around their waists. The thin little boys shrieked with laughter as they hopped into the hewn oak log trough and began to jump up and down on the hides to soften them. "They will be doing this for some time to make it pliable."

"I know nothing of leather making." I looked at the olive-skinned boys with pity, but it appeared like they were having fun.

"I pay these boys a fair wage to stomp the skins. These two are orphans." The boys waved at Simon and grinned when he spoke.

"You are a good man, Simon. I won't keep you from your work, eh. Show me some shoe leather to trade with the cobblers, and we will be on our way." They walked to a small storage nearby to see Simon's finished hides. Zeke selected some leather pieces, secured them in a sturdy leather sack he placed on his donkey's back.

I went to the house to thank Elena who was sitting out front on a mat and combing her long dark hair. Sea breezes lifted her shiny tresses and tossed them about as she attempted to tame them. She rose to give me cheek kisses and tried to say in Aramaic, "Come again."

"I will," I said and gave her the filled flask. Zeke joined me in thanking them for their hospitality, and we left.

We continued on the trail by the Great Sea. The air was clear and crisp the first day but became overcast the next morning. We traveled to Caesarea Maritima. As we approached, Zeke said, "It is a port, a base for the Herodian navy. The Emperor, Augustus Caesar, had an aqueduct built to bring water to the town."

I had never seen such structures as were here, and asked, "Where does the water in the aqueduct come from? What are these buildings?"

Zeke chuckled, "When you ask many questions, I think you must be enjoying the trek, eh. The water comes from springs about sixteen kilometers away, eh. These buildings are a combination of Greek and Roman style, rather different from what you normally see, eh. I would like to take you to the area of Mount Hermon, to Caesarea Philippi, where the Jordan River begins. It will take us three or four days to walk, and more if we stop to rest or sell rugs."

"I would like to see it, I think."

We traveled for days and made some stops. One morning Zeke sensed some danger as his donkeys balked. One of them brayed and stomped his front hoof. We did not move onward. "Something is making them afraid to go." He listened, so I knew to remain as quiet as a statue.

We were like four statues there on the trail for what

felt to me like an eternity. One donkey switched his tail before he began to walk. He nodded as if to his fellow donkey, and we all resumed our trek. I breathed a sigh, and Zeke nodded with a smile.

"No doubt they smelled a mountain lion, but it moved on. We must be vigilant." The remainder of the day was uneventful.

As we climbed up the Southwestern slope of Mount Herman to the city of Caesarea Philippi on a large plateau, I was awed and elated. I had wondered what the birds saw as they looked down from their skyward journeys. From this vantage point, I had a glimpse of their view, and I loved it. Rising in the city was a white marble temple. I was fascinated by everything. Upon seeing the grotto and the headwaters of a river flowing, I asked, "Where does this water come from and where does it go?"

"It is the beginning of the Jordan River, eh. Water inside the earth feeds it, so it spews forth. Soon we will see some carvings. Long ago this was a shrine to Baal and Pan. Philip the tetrarch has created this city with pools and gardens. From here the view of the surrounding area is vastly broad, eh. It is called Caesarea Philippi, in honor of the emperor Tiberius."

"I have heard about Baal worship, but who is Pan?"
"He is Greek, eh. In ancient times, people who came to this place thought it resembled their country so they settled here and claimed it to be the birthplace of Pan, their god."

"Does Our Lord know this Pan?" I had not heard of any other except false desert gods. I was tired and wanted to rest, but did not want to stay near a foreign god. Clouds gathered in the sky, creating a feeling of gloomy impending weather change.

Zeke chuckled. "The Almighty One, whose name you cannot say, knows everything, eh. According to the Greeks, Pan was in charge of nature, fields, forests, mountains, flocks, and probably shepherds."

"You are right. I suppose the Lord does know everything. He has spared this old widow from the grave, and I am ready for the next adventure."

"You are not old, eh. My years far outnumber yours. I think we will spend time on the trail to Jerusalem, and when I have finished my business there, I will return to the coastal trail."

Rain drenched us, but my spirit was not dampened. We trekked without incident to Jerusalem. The temple, with its surroundings, appeared before me as majestic as ever. Zeke bartered for a second donkey and loaded it with honey, wine, Simon's leather, and grain to trade for rugs. Zeke was happy to have me listen to his travel tales and cook his meals. I enjoyed the trip, but became weary and longed to see Marian.

Next stop for him would be to Sidon where Zeke planned to travel by boat to Paphos on the island of Cyprus. He would cross the waters to Myra to meet traders from the east who had silks, jewelry, rugs, pottery, and other fine wares.

"How is Tabitha, eh? You seem to have your mind in a distant place."

"I thought I wanted to go far away, but I am sad. I miss my daughter." I dreamed of how it would be at home in my little hut with Marian and my friend Lottie nearby. "The unbreakable thread I seek is not as important as her."

"It is right to miss those you love, eh." He gazed toward the distant hills but told me nothing of his family. I wondered if he had lost loved ones. We continued on in silence with the two donkeys clopping and our sandals echoing. He had offered to let me ride on a donkey, but he was walking so I walked beside him.

It had been a long, interesting journey for me, but I could think of nothing except my daughter and wanted to go home. While we were in Lydda, Zeke left me alone with one of the donkeys to watch over the items he had to trade. I was sorely tempted to leave. I sat in the shade of an olive tree with branches laden with ripened fruit and whose trunk was large and gnarled. Olives were going to waste on the ground. I patted it, wondering at its age, and named it Methuselah. "Lord, what shall I do? My life is a broken thread. I do not know if you hear a woman's voice, yet I plead. How many days do I have in my life, and what do you want me to do with them?" Even though the disciple of the rabbi told me God had blessed me when I gave my last coins, I still doubted a distant Lord heard me.

When Zeke returned, I said, "I have seen many wonders traveling with you, yet I yearn to see Marian and be home. You know I have no money, but if there is anything I can do to repay you for feeding me, I will."

"You do not owe me one coin. I have enjoyed having you to talk with and help me cook, and I will miss you." He smiled and looked away for a short while. "I will accompany you home, eh?" When he looked at me, I thought I saw tears glistening in his eyes.

"No, I think I can make it as I know the route from here. You need to be on your way this season before the waves leap up to devour you when you cross the sea."

He walked with me until we came to the trail to my home and stayed until he was satisfied I could make it the rest of the way. It was daylight, and he traveled on after watering the donkeys. Zeke walked away, looked back at me from time to time. I waved to him and brushed my tears. The days now had less sun as it stole away sooner than before. I wanted to hurry home.

I found myself hoping Uzziah was not at home but shook my head as I remembered he was no longer a threat. Although a little frightened to be on my own, I was determined to be brave as I watched Zeke fade from view. My father had told me the strength of spirit inside a person could get them through the toughest times. And Mother had shown me how to tie a broken thread and continue on.

I was close to my home, but my wobbly legs felt like they could not go another step, and my eyes were half-closed. I found an olive tree shadow and spread my cloak to lie down for a moment before I faced my hut and memories. A pleasant breeze lulled me to sleep. A voice startled me. "Tabitha, I have work for you to do."

Fear clutched my chest, and I could not speak. "What work?" I answered the Voice I could not see. I trembled, wondering what this meant. He had used the name I desired. "Did you call me Tabitha?"

"Yes, child. You shall leap forward and help widows."

"My mother is taken care of by my sisters."

"You must go to Joppa."

"Why? What will I do? Am I to find unbroken thread?"

"It takes three. The Lord will provide." A breeze wafted over me and all was quiet as I awakened, dazed, and hoping I could trust the voice in the dream as I remembered every word. I had work to do, but I was not sure how to begin. I was perplexed by the words, "It takes three." Three strands of thread would be thicker than the eye of a needle. If it were much finer spun thread, it would break anyway. What could it mean?

The glory of the sun sank over the side of the earth from the blue heavens as I neared my hut. My nap had been disturbing, and I was eager to see my home again. During my last few steps, I pondered the message from the unseen visitor. Whether it was a dream or real, I was inspired by the thought of helping women in need. Perhaps it was a reason to go on living.

Happy tears glistened when I saw my home stood

as it had before I left. Once inside, I saw it was a little dustier. I wondered how Marian was doing, yet I decided to wait until the morning to go see her. Mice had left their dirt in place of any crumbs of meal on the floor. I swept, but dust waited to be wiped from shelves and table. It felt good to be home, dusting and sweeping. Uzziah's death made me feel guilty in spite of my atonement gift, but I no longer had to worry about him.

I heard people talking a short distance away when I awakened in the morning and decided it was travelers getting water and refreshing themselves. My curiosity led me to open the door. I saw a cart with horses, and people were drawing water from the well. I decided not to go greet the travelers as I had nothing to feed them. I turned and went inside to finish dusting.

At last, my hut was clean. I gathered my staff and bag and hurried down the trail to see Marian and Lottie. My life pulse raced and my feet matched its pace as I was excited to see my daughter.

Lottie welcomed me with open arms. "What a surprise. You have been gone so long, I thought you might not return." Lottie's forehead was creased as if with pain or worry. "Are you well? Did Zeke mistreat you? Is he living with you?"

"So many questions. I am all right and tired, but you also look weary. No, Zeke is not living with me. He was a good companion and brother who provided for me on our journey." I caught my breath. "It was an exciting trip, and I saw wonderful places I will tell you about. I returned because I was lonesome for Marian and home, and you too." We embraced, kissed cheeks.

"Why did you not stay with him? He could provide for you." Lottie held my arms, studied my face. She had a strained look in her eyes.

"What is wrong? How are things with you?" An ache in my bosom longed for my daughter who had not come running to me. Dread tightened my throat as I asked, "Where is Marian?"

Seventeen

He awakened inside a cart, wedged between the carriage wall and old Elias. Perspiration stinks mingled with the odors of women and children wafted into his nostrils. A young child kept up a constant clatter of talking and giggling. How had he come to be inside the cart? His mind focused on the attack and his failure to defend himself. Thoughts crept into his mind and then poured like a stream: thankful to be whole in spite of head pain, thankful to be safe, and wonderment at being alive. Why had they not left him behind?

"Uzziah." Silas threaded his way among legs to get closer. "How do you feel?"

"Doing well, I think." He shook his head. "My legs are dead."

"You were snuffed out like the last coal of a fire. I tried to drag you to the cart, but Father and Horatio lifted you in. You were the main casualty. I think your legs are only sleeping."

"Thank you for not leaving me for dead. No one hurt, then?"

"We would not leave a guest as Mother believes any stranger could be an angel."

It took a moment to speak as Uzziah eyed his blue, naked finger where his signet ring had been torn away. "I am no angel."

"I like you anyway." Silas clapped him on the shoulder.

"You are a true friend, Silas. You will grow up to be a fine man."

"What brought you to us? What did you do before, and why do you not go back?"

"Silas." His mother called firmly.

"Yes, Mother." Silas stood and turned around. "We will talk again."

As the trail wended on, they traveled to Jacob's Well and trekked beside the Jordan River. Mount Gerazim loomed on one side and the water flowed and whooshed as a constant companion most days. They made their way on the low trail, not the mountain.

The family was kind and lived in harmony with their servants. The mother was from Judah, and she believed in the God of Abraham. Wills had said nothing about his belief. One day Uzziah asked, "Do you go to the temple on the Holy Days?"

Wills scratched his beard and looked away. "I do not trust any god or have faith in the One Lord as does my wife. I believe in myself and my own wisdom to get by." He looked at Uzziah. "Are you able to take your turn at the reins now?"

The Jordan pulsed nearby like a live animal breathing on and on. He took the reins, and was quiet, deep in thought. There was a chill in the air.

They stopped to rest, and Wills' wife brought out a casting net. She and Silas went into the water a little way and were fishing. Uzziah watched for a while and thought to go along, but he knew nothing about fishing. Silas begged, "Come down and help. We want to catch fish for our meal."

Since he was taking advantage of their hospitality, Uzziah was pleased to help cast the net and draw up a few fish. They sloshed out of the water and cleaned and skinned the catch with practiced hands.

Uzziah took the reins again when they moved on. Silas crept out of the cart and climbed up to him. "Remember what we were talking about when you first woke up in the cart?"

Uzziah kept steady with the reins and gazed as if there were something out on the horizon he did not want to miss. At last, he said, "Silas, I made some bad choices. I had an older brother of whom I was always jealous. I was not treated terribly, but I was sure my father did not love me as much as him. My mother always comforted me when I cried as a boy. When I got older, I turned to strong drink, mostly wine, to make me feel good. I went to the city, spent money, and usually got drunk. It did not always go well."

Silas hopped down and kept walking beside him. "Where is your brother?"

"He died a few years ago."

"Oh, I am sorry. Did you inherit all the land your father gave to him?"

"I did. Working the land was difficult since my father had not taught me well, and it was an ongoing laborious process year after year. You may not understand it, but we lost it to Roman taxation."

"You said, we, does that mean you had another brother?"

"No, I had Jacob's wife after he died. Taking care of your brother's widow is a responsibility in our faith."

Silas mused over the information. His brow knitted and he said, "I should see if Mother needs me for anything." He hoisted himself into the cart.

Uzziah spent many happy days in their company. Time was unimportant, but he knew they had gone through cooler weather and it was springtime. He could tell the family was poor as they had no land, only their cart and the donkeys. The women made scarves, jewelry, and small trinkets. The family bartered and traded for other goods. Some items they used, but others were traded for more money later in their travels. While an occasional argument took place, singing and general peace created a sense of deep happiness. Wills' and Horatio's wives were great cooks, and everyone ate well. They always had enough food.

Soon his surroundings took on a familiarity. It was as if at any moment he would see his father, brother, or neighbor on the trail. So much had changed for Uzziah. He did not want to be a burden to Wills and his family. He mused to himself that he had been dead twice, or could have been. The neglected barley crop rolled before him like the Jordan. No fresh planting had been done. Weeds towered here and there among the depleted stalks of grain.

"We should water the donkeys. Do you know of any well nearby?" Wills asked. "You were in yonder area by the trail behind the brushy hill when we met."

"I do know a well. We can all rest and get a drink." He felt chills all over and wanted to escape, not from Wills, but the past.

When they reached the well, Silas exclaimed, "Look, there is a small house. I wonder who lives in it."

"Do not venture there. You must help lead the horses to the trough." Wills helped his wife out of the cart.

Uzziah hoped he would see Meydl Tabitha but feared what would happen if he saw her and confronted her.

Wills and his wife cleaned the cooking utensils. He lifted the heavy crockery for her, and she scrubbed it. They did not look up while Uzziah watched, envious of the easy companionship they had. He wondered if he was ready to pursue life without them.

Many events along the way taught Uzziah skills he

had not learned in a lifetime at home. Wills had shown him how to make a fire without flint, using sticks. Silas found berries, greens, bird eggs, and bugs good for food. Horatio taught him to lead donkeys as well as horses to pull the carriage. He watched him create utensils, bowls, stirrers, and trinkets from wood. Most helpful was Wills' wife who asked him to help her with the net when she fished. They had all taught by their example of kindness, forgiveness, and the joy of being together.

"Wills, I do not have the words to thank you for all you, your family, and servants have done. Nor can I thank your wife enough for the healing balm applied to my wounds when I needed help." He approached his benefactor, still uncertain about what he would do.

"Uzziah, you are no trouble at all and have been a great help for us. I hope you will travel on with us."

"My time with you has been an experience I will never forget. You saved my life. I am not far from my home and can find my way from here."

"Is yours the hut I see on the other side of this vineyard?" Silas was at his elbow and had seen Uzziah staring at it. "You could run there to visit quickly then catch up with us again."

"No." A catch in his voice stifled words. He looked down at the adoring, sad face and realized the boy had become like a younger brother might be. He grasped the boy's shoulders. "I have to go home to my family, Silas. I have been away many months, and they need me."

Silas stood on tiptoe and kissed his cheeks. "Uzziah, you are my best friend."

"You are like a brother to me. Grow up to be the man you were meant to be." When Uzziah kissed his cheeks, they were wet. Silas kissed both his cheeks again. He let go of him and turned to Wills and the others as they all bid their goodbyes.

"My father and the two little ones are asleep," Wills said, and he grasped his arms with strong hands. "Go with your gods."

"Travel safely. I will miss all of you, but I must . . ." He lost words.

"We understand you need to put your life to rights as best you can," Wills said. He turned toward the carriage as the family settled to travel.

Uzziah stepped into the small vineyard and meandered among the vines until he heard the horses clopping and the wheels crunching the earth as they moved. His thoughts were scattered like grains strewed for planting. Would Meydl Tabitha take him back? He thought not as she would loathe to allow him in. Perhaps he could go away and learn a trade to provide for her and Marian. What would he do? He had enjoyed fishing as they had done along the way in rivers and streams. It was great fun and fresh food, but there was no stream nearby.

His mother had told him his grandfather was a fisherman, and about their family, the town and the sea, but he was not paying much attention then. He walked on the familiar path to the gray and white hut.

At the sight of the small mean replacement of his father's house, a coldness seeped into his heart. He began to rage inside at her carelessness. It was an insult to the memory of his parent's existence and land. She was a terrible woman to leave him nothing at all. Despair and anger rose in him. His nostrils flared, blurred all else from his mind, and removed all rational thought. He had once loved her as passionately as he now hated her. He hated Jacob, hated him for dying and leaving them all helpless.

Uzziah stood at the door. He wanted to punish her! His clenched fist was ready. When he heard no sound from inside, Uzziah came into the hut. He was angry with his wife for not being there. He saw his sleeping mat rolled in the corner of the room. Meydl was infuriatingly neat. She wanted him to call her Tabitha, but he thought of her as Meydl, the girl he met on the trail so long ago. There was no dust on any surface. He would sit and wait, give her a sound beating when she returned.

He heard footsteps outside, and he leaped up, ready. The door opened as with a tentative hand. Why did she not enter? He stood with clenched fists. "Come in," he yelled.

"Do not be angry." Silas poked his head in. His eyes squinted.

"Silas, what are you doing here?" Uzziah's hands dangled at his sides, defeated.

"I did not want to leave you unless you were really

going home."

"Go back. Your mother will be worried something bad happened to you."

"You have a nice little place. I want to stay with you." Silas came inside. His young eyes looked up at Uzziah, pleading to be heard.

"No, you must not. They cannot have gone far. Let us both run and catch up with them." He knew he must act fast. He did not want to have Wills angry with Silas or him. Uzziah grabbed the boy's hand and went out, shutting the door. They trotted along the trail and saw the faint dust cloud as the carriage crept to a stop. Wills raced toward them and met them halfway.

Wills clutched his son's hand. He reached into his pouch and pulled out a thin leather strap, tied one end to his wrist and the other to Silas' wrist. There was a fierce look of love in his eyes and the grim appearance of fatherly duty written on his face.

Some brief words of thanks were murmured to Uzziah, and he walked away. He was struck by memories of his father and the punishment he meted out. Could it be he had missed his father's love in all the times he had tried to teach him and set rules for his behavior?

He went to the vineyard and randomly pulled at the haphazard, gnarled vines. Perhaps he could retake the neglected property his family had lost. Of course, he did not know how he would begin to negotiate it. He kept walking, no longer ready to encounter his woman. She probably thought he was dead, and would she not be surprised when she saw him? He would someday follow through with his revenge. He wanted to show her what an evil thing she had done to leave him dying, a feast for animals. He balled his fist and slammed it into his other palm.

Eighteen

e took Marian to Ekron. She is with a healer who is caring for her," Lottie said. She put her arm about my shoulder and said, "Do not worry."

"What is it? What happened to make her ill?" Stricken with fear, I screamed "Oh, my Marian."

"Be calm. Marian became a woman with her moon cycle, and we gave thanks with her to celebrate her womanhood. Yet, for two months the bleeding continued painfully and would not stop. Our neighbor told us about the healer Serena. She was formerly with a nomadic shepherd tribe and has settled in Ekron with her husband Philip, the metal worker."

"I want to go see Marian." I was grieved I had not been there to care for her. I was a terrible mother to have abandoned my daughter at this age. "Ekron is not far." I turned to go.

"We will both go." Lottie held onto my shoulder.

"I see you survived, dear neighbor." Samuel strode in.

"Yes, I will tell you all about it later, but I must go see my Marian."

Samuel looked at Lottie who had grabbed her cloak. He shook his head and rubbed his moist forehead. "Give me a short time, and I will go with you women."

My anxiety grew as I did not want to delay. He went out to inform servants to tend cattle but was ready by the time Mia had gotten everything together in a sack Lottie wanted to bring along.

The walk was three hours, and the sun was high in the sky. When we arrived at Serena's place, I did not wait for anyone to answer the door. Marian reclined on cushions, and she leaped to her feet to meet me. "Mother, oh, what a joy to see you. I missed you so." We clung to each other, crying happy tears. "Did Lottie tell you?"

"Yes, I am overjoyed you have reached womanhood but worried because you became ill. How are you doing now?"

"I have had no issue for three days. Serena says I can go home, eat vegetables, and take an herbal tea she will send with me." Marian reddened as Samuel stood in the doorway looking as if he wanted to escape.

"I will visit Philip in his metal shop." Samuel went out.

Marian hugged Lottie. "I am glad you came and

brought my mother. Serena was going to have a servant go to get you tomorrow. Mother, oh I cannot tell you how much it means to see you." She reached for my hand and clung to it.

"Hello everyone," Serena said. She was a tall, older woman who walked with an erect posture. Her hair was shiny white with brown streaks, and braided into a coil that formed a crown on her head.

"I really liked being with Serena. I want to be a healer like her." Marian's voice was animated as she went to her benefactor, who put an arm around her shoulders.

"Marian, I have enjoyed your company too." Serena patted Marian's back.

"It would be a useful skill." Lottie smiled.

"I am very thankful to you, Serena. My daughter has been cared for with your expert healing arts." I wondered what payment was owed.

"Samuel will pay you," said Lottie.

"You owe me nothing. Marian has earned her keep by helping me organize my shelves of herbs and doing small chores for me. If you do wish to allow her to learn healing arts, I am happy to be her teacher. Marian is quick to catch on to anything I have shown her. She and I get along so well, she will surely earn her way by assisting me."

"Mother, may I please?" Marian looked at me with large pleading eyes and turned to Lottie. "Mother Lottie?"

Lottie nodded.

"Do you truly want to do this?" I took Marian's hands in mine.

"Yes, but I will go home with you for a few days before I begin as I have missed you and want to hear of your adventures."

"You may work with her if you have your heart set on it. Thank you again, Serena. You are a miracle worker."

"I look forward to having Marian with me so I can pass on my healing knowledge to her. It will be a joy to have her helping me, and to teach her to be my assistant." She smiled and nodded. "She may take over for me someday."

"I could not ever take your place. Thank you for all you did for me." Marian and Serena embraced and kissed cheeks. "And Mother Lottie, thank you for bringing me here."

"Yes, I appreciate you and Samuel bringing Marian to Serena," I said.

"It was what I knew we had to do." Lottie brought us both into her ample embrace.

After refreshing ourselves with water from an urn, we bid farewell to Serena and met Samuel outside to make our trip home before dark. He had come from Philip's metal-working shop. "Are you women ready to go?"

"We are, but we have Marian with us who has been ill."

As we began our trek, our shadows were small dark pools at our feet. We needed to walk slower with Marian, and I feared we would not return by sunset.

On the trail, we kept up a good pace for a time, and Samuel said, "Let us take our rest by the dry creek in the shade of those trees. We do not want to tire Marian."

We sat in the shade. Marian said, "Thank you, I wish the water was there so I could cool my feet."

"As would I." Lottie rolled her eyes and settled beside Samuel.

Samuel looked toward me, "I may as well tell you this now. We have found a suitable husband for Marian if you approve."

My daughter sucked in her breath.

"Well, thank you. Who is the fortunate young man?" I was surprised, as they had not discussed it with me.

"Not young. He is a widower, Azel, a successful landowner."

"Oh, I know the man. He has the olive press." Jacob had dealt with him many times, paying him to press our olive crop into oil. I was surprised by the choice, as Azel was a widower nearly my age.

"He is a kind man," Lottie said. "And has much to offer a wife."

"Does he have children?" Marian asked.

"A son and daughter who are both married."

"The rest of his children and his wife died some years ago." Samuel stood, dusted dry leaves from his clothes with his hands, and grabbed his staff. We all continued on the trail.

We walked in silence. Marian looked at me and shrugged. My thoughts whirled about in my head. I wondered if Azel would allow her to learn to be a healer. I thought about my own life and the work I had been called to do.

We arrived as the sun was sinking from the rim of the earth and deep shadows were cast. Marian and I went to our home. I had an odd feeling someone had been inside my house, and I remembered the cart of people at the well I had not greeted. Perhaps someone had stepped inside to see if anyone was home. I was ill at ease and could not drowse at first. Many troubling memories of Uzziah crept into my head, and I could not quiet them. At last, my exhaustion bested me, and I slept with Marian curled asleep on a mat next to me.

The following days we discussed Marian's wedding plans. She was not against marrying an older man. He had fields, groves, and an olive press, and would provide for her. Since he was older, she thought he would demand little of her attention and allow her to learn healing arts from Serena. I wanted to tell her not to make any assumptions until she had met her future husband, but I said nothing. I knew he was a good and devout man who had gone to Jerusalem to worship with Jacob many times.

"I will go with you, Lottie and Samuel, to arrange for the betrothal if you are in agreement with Samuel's choice."

"After I meet the man, I will let you know," said Marian.

"You are fortunate to have a parent like me. Girls are not allowed to decide who their husband will be." I looked earnestly into my daughter's eyes, wanting the best for her. She nodded and hugged me.

The meeting was arranged with Azel. He was short in stature, a kind, gray-haired, agreeable man who spoke well. I wondered how he had escaped the Roman taxation and kept his land. He walked with a limp but otherwise was able-bodied. Gifts were discussed. I insisted they go to Samuel because he had acted in place of her father. A year betrothal was agreed upon.

"Marian, why did you not ask about the possibility of learning healing arts?" I implored, once we were alone in our hut.

"I will wait until the time is right. He will agree, I think."

"Why do you think so?"

"He smiled on me like Samuel who has usually let me do as I wish." Marian pouted her lips, grinned, and lifted her shoulder playfully.

"Samuel and Lottie have treated you like a princess." I picked up a towel and pretended to strike her with it. I laughed.

"Mother, I am not spoiled." Marian giggled and grabbed the towel from me.

"You are as tall as I am, and you have become a lovely young woman. Besides, you have a keen mind, and I am very proud of you." The two of us basked in the warmth of each other's company for several days. My rest did not last long.

Nineteen

I awakened feeling clammy with perspiration. The voice once again had come to me. "Tabitha, make haste and go to Joppa where you are sorely needed." I did not know how I would answer the call, but I knew I must. I thought about the voice calling me Tabitha because there was no doubt it spoke directly to me. What if it was a strange dream and I was wrong? Father had told stories about God calling people to action. If it was the Lord, I was humbled and pleased he had called me, and I felt I must answer him.

After Marian and I spent more days together, I knew it was time to go away. She was sitting in the sunshine stitching on a scarf. I gazed at my beautiful daughter and wondered at being blessed with such a precious gift. In my heart and mind, I knew I was being called to leave her. All mothers must separate from their children, even as at birth the cord is severed, so when they are grown, we give them their freedom from our clutching arms. They will not stray too far we hope, and voluntarily come back, perhaps, and care for us when we age. I sat beside her and put my arm around her shoulder. "I have loved spending all these days with you, but I have had a call in a dream urging me to go to Joppa and help widows."

She stopped embroidering the leaf, breathed a sigh, looked into my eyes, and said, "Mother, I want you to stay, but I cannot stop you from doing what you feel you have to do. The Lord, whose name we do not say, may have put the desire in you to do good works."

"You are right, Marian, I believe it is the Lord. I am happy you are understanding of my urgency to heed the call. I feared you would think I had a sickness in my mind. I do not know what I will do to help the widows, but I must."

She smiled and said, "Mother, I know what you will do. You can sew clothing."

"You are right. I will need material and thread, and if it is what I am supposed to do, I believe the Lord will provide. The last time he spoke to me in a dream he made a comment about it taking three, and I do not understand the meaning."

"I do not want you to go, but I can see how important it is to you. Please come before my wedding." Her eyes pleaded. "I am doing well with Mother Lottie, and I know she has missed me these few days I have been with you. I will be busy with my wedding plans if I am allowed to participate."

I walked with Marian to Lottie and Samuel's home and kissed her goodbye. Lottie was smiling, "I am happy to have my Marian back, but I am sorry you think you must leave again."

"I will return in time for the wedding." I hugged Marian, envious of the relationship Lottie had with my daughter. It was a closeness I would have enjoyed more if circumstances were different. The three of us were tearful as I prepared to leave.

"I do not want you to trek alone." Lottie held me at arms-length and looked me in the eye. Before I could speak, she said, "Samuel will ask a servant to attend you." Lottie motioned toward Mia, who had heard her, and she ran out to the field where Samuel worked.

"I do not want to be a burden." I frowned but knew it was useless to protest. When she came in, we talked about Marian's care and her upcoming wedding. In a short time, Sheaf, a trusted servant stood waiting to take my pack and follow me. Lottie and I clasped arms, kissed teary cheeks, and Marion joined in, hugging me tightly. We let go, and I did not look back lest I lose my determination to serve others as I had been bidden.

I carried my last bread crust and a flask of water and wine mixture. I shook my head, remembering bitterly how I was not able to keep wine in my house when Uzziah was alive. I brought a half-finished plain tunic. I fought the fear and the tears plaguing me and urging me to turn around. When I looked up at the expanse of blue sky, I was a mere speck of dust to the Creator of everything. Yet he must have sent his messenger in the dream to watch over me as I listened and obeyed.

As Sheaf and I walked, we stopped to rest at the dry creek shade trees. I welcomed the opportunity to sit a few moments. He stayed a respectful distance. I heard a noise and presumed it to be Sheaf, but when I looked up, I did not see anything. My life pulse raced, and I stood on shaky legs and called, "Sheaf."

Sheaf came running to me to see why I had summoned him. "Yes, what is it?'

"It was the rustling of an animal, probably nothing."

"We go." He picked up my pack, grabbed my hand, and we walked apace until we had gone a way down the trail. He bowed. "I hope you were not offended as I took your hand without asking, but I felt we had to move fast. Are you well?"

"Yes." I caught my breath and heaved a sigh of relief. I was nervous about the trip, and it had caused me to react to the sounds I heard.

Except for moonlight, it was dark when we reached the home of Simon the tanner, and the place stank as I expected. I was wearied from traveling and was hopeful Simon and Elena would give me a place to rest until I could find another.

Simon was removing the last hairs from a hide and turned to see me approach in the moonlit night. "Hello, what brings you to my humble home?"

Sheaf gave me my pack and waved when he saw I spoke with Simon.

"I do not know if you remember me. Many days ago, I came with Zeke the Rug Man."

"Yes, yes, I do recall," Simon said, scratched his head, and shook it from side to side. "Your name is Meydl?"

"Yes, Simon, yet I am named Meydl Tabitha for my mother, who is dead since my birth. I wish to be called by her name."

"Your mother lives in you. Tabitha is a good name, and I shall not forget it. Let me take you to Elena. She will enjoy having company." He wiped his hands on a rag and carried my pack.

When we neared his home, I thought it looked like a ship silhouetted against the backdrop of the moon glow on the dark green sea. I hoped it would prove to be a haven in the midst of my uncertain life.

"Simon, you have brought me a friend." Elena opened the door and we kissed cheeks. "Welcome. Come sit and have some tea with me." She said this in her language, waved her hands expressively and pointed to the water boiling on the hearth. She dropped in a scoop of tea leaves from a hanging sack. A spicy orange aroma perfumed the air inside the house.

"Meydl? Tabitha?" As she waited for the tea, Elena looked at me, trying to recall my name.

"Yes, she has taken her mother's name Tabitha. It is also a graceful antelope, Dorcas to you," Simon said, as he opened the door, and gave a slight wave of his hand. "I will go wash up and leave you ladies to your tea."

Elena beamed a smile at me as I untied my small sack and flasks from my waist. We sat cross-legged on a mat on the floor as we drank tea. I decided to try to communicate with Elena by pointing to things and saying the word in Aramaic. "Tea," I said.

"Tea," Elena repeated, and she said the name in her language. We made a game of it, sometimes with Elena pointing to an object and saying its name. I would then pronounce my word in Aramaic. We did some common words before we started testing each other's memory of the ones we had learned. She smiled and we laughed together. I supped with them, and they insisted I stay.

I remained with my new friends. The stench of the hides was usually driven away from their house by a fresh sea breeze. I was not sure where I would continue to live, nor did I know how I was to help the widows of Joppa. I slept fitfully with the dilemma troubling me. When I awakened Simon was at work.

Elena had stepped outside, so I was alone with my thoughts. "Lord, I am here, waiting for more direction." I wondered if I was disillusioned, and the distant Lord had not spoken to me at all. I did not expect an answer. I went to the well for some water to wash up and heard the distant swish of the sea lapping the bank. The soothing sound calmed me with an abiding peace. I stayed outside enjoying the sunshine and sea breeze, held my nose, and walked over to watch Simon. "Good day to you."

"Good day. I hope you slept well. "

"I did and I am enjoying word games with Elena."

"I am happy you two are talking. I know it stinks here, but you are welcome to stay with us as long as you like. You are good company for Elena, as few women venture here for reasons your nose knows. I do not smell anything when I work, as I have done it all my life." He gave a little laugh and continued. "Zeke stopped by and gave us a large sack of materials for sewing and some yarns for weaving. In truth, I did not look inside the bag, but he said a clever woman could turn its contents into clothing. Elena does not sew or weave, and we were wondering if you would have some use for it."

"Oh, I would like very much to have some fabrics to sew garments." I squealed with excitement. A gift of fabric was my first affirmation of what I was supposed to do in Joppa. It had been some time since I had one new piece of material let alone many. The Lord had answered my plea. "I sew, and I can weave if I have a loom. I cannot believe my good fortune. My father used to tell me God provides for his people. I am grateful to you for giving me sewing to do, something I enjoy. I will sew for others in need."

"The Lord Almighty does give good gifts. I learned how to make leather from my father, and he from my grandfather, so I have a business and trade because of them." Simon stood, straightened his back for a moment before he bent and continued to scrape a hide.

"I will go to see if Elena needs my help."

"Ask her to show you the bag of material."

When I went into the house, the aroma of fish cooking filled the air. Elena was at the hearth stirring a pot of soup. "Did you sleep well?" Elena pointed to my rolled mat in the corner, so I could tell what she meant.

"Yes." I paused, groped for a way illustrate, closed my eyes and smiled, nodding my head.

"Fish stew with herbs," Elena said, pointing to the pot. She took some spoons from a cloth wherein they were wrapped and ladled some broth into a bowl for me to taste.

"Umm, it is good," I said, after tasting the warm broth.

"Umm, it is good," repeated Elena. First, she said it in Aramaic, then Koine.

We both laughed. I thought my life was going well. I missed Lottie, but I had a new friend. I took out my pack with the unfinished tunic and showed it to Elena. "I sew garments. Zeke left some materials like this." I held it up. Elena knew what I was saying and went to get the sack of cloth.

When I spread the fabric on the clean-swept floor, I was amazed at the colors and types. There were tan, white, and yellow linens, brown, purple, plain, and red cottons. Along with a silk piece dyed with many colors like a rainbow, these fabrics were to my seamstress hands like food to a hungry person. I had not owned such an array and never had seen this many kind of cloth except in the booths at the market in Jerusalem.

Tears of joy filled my eyes, and I hugged my new friend. "I do love these."

"Take all," Elena said. "I do not sew." She shook her head from side to side and made a sewing motion with her hand as if she had a needle and was attempting to ply it.

"Thank you," I said, "I will make a new dress for you." I laid out a tan-colored length of linen and a red cotton piece. Some thread was wound on sticks and would serve to sew the clothes. "Choose one, or any of the others." I gestured.

She pointed to the red cotton and said the color in her language.

I could not be happier. I had sewing to do and a new friend with whom I was learning to communicate. Everything was going well, and I continued to stay, although not sure when I would know the widows I was to help.

Elena was in tears as I walked into the kitchen one morning. I smelled something had scorched, "Are you hurt? What can I do?"

She pointed to a burnt loaf of bread on the table and through hand gestures told me she had forgotten it when she was tending to other household chores.

"It is a shame, but not such a great loss. I will help you make more." I lifted a portion of flour from the bin and put it in a large bowl. I added water from a pitcher, but I was missing the usual sour leavening, a yeast given to me by my mother. "Where is the yeast?"

She understood what I needed as she had dried her eyes and watched me. She handed me a dish from her windowsill. It was a frothy gray mixture and smelled right. I smiled at her and poured some of it into the bowl of flour and water, stirred it in with a spoon. I took some of the mixture and stirred it into the yeast pot. Next, I added more flour into the bowl, and a little sea salt and kneaded it with my hands until it was a shiny mass of dough. "Now we will let it rise before we shape it into rounds."

"Good friend," Elena said, grasping for the words to thank me. "You made bread dough."

"Bread dough."

"Bread dough," she repeated in Aramaic. We both laughed, eager to continue learning words.

"Hello." Simon came inside the house, ready to have his breakfast. When he saw the blackened bread, he shook his head, went to Elena, and put his arm around her shoulders. "It will be okay. We will not starve." Pots of cheese and one cheese wheel were on a shelf. He took down a pot of cheese, put a knife into the bread, and cut out the center away from the burnt crust.

It was a quality I admired in Simon. He was kind to his wife and tried to make the best of any situation. He cut another piece of bread and smeared it with soft cheese, and offered it to Elena and me. It tasted a little charred but was not unpleasant. After he finished eating bread and some dried fruits, he went back to work.

When I was stitching the garment for Elena from the red cotton cloth, I experienced satisfaction. She had gone outside, so I decided to take my sewing basket and join her. She held a torn tunic, and I showed her how to repair it. We continued talking, and I learned a lot of words she regularly used. It was not only wonderful for me to have a new language to learn and teach, but more importantly, a friend. Time passed as we filled our days getting to know each other. We were carrying on a conversation and I was sewing as she was mending Simon's tunic. The normal quietness was disturbed as we heard men's rumbling voices coming from Simon's work area. It sounded like an argument, but I could not hear what they said. I looked at Elena. "Do you know who it might be? Is it Simon and a customer?"

Elena shook her head and put down her project. She stood, looking in the direction of the rumbling animated voices. I joined her at the door and saw some men near Simon. One seemed to be jumping up and down in anger, and the other was crouched as if to pounce. "I will go see," she said.

"I will come along in case you need help."

Twenty

s we approached Simon, he had stopped working and was standing by with an amused look on his face listening to two young men argue.

"James, why must you break rules? You are an idiot," yelled a man in a travel-worn tunic.

"Same to ya, ya dumb fish." The man looked a lot like the first, and he was red-faced with anger. "Father Zebedee did not give me anything before we left. Ya think he favors me. Search my cloak if ya want." He raised his fist. "I oughta throw ya in the stinking trough."

"We were told by Jesus not to take anything with us, but you had something in your waist pouch. I know it."

"Prove it."

"I will see." He lunged toward him, and the two of them wrestled on the ground, oblivious of their audience.

"Boys, boys," Simon chided. "There are women present, and you are shamefully exposing your legs."

The young men stopped fighting and rolled away from each other.

"James, John, this is Tabitha. You remember Elena."

"I am pleased to meet you. Sorry, we did not know you were here," said John, blushing behind his ample beard, and lowering his eyes.

"I'm also pleased to meet ya," said James, as he dusted himself off.

"Come have some wine and bread when you sons of thunder have settled down and washed," Simon said. Elena smiled and nodded.

As Elena and I walked to the house, I realized I had not thought about the bad stink of the tanning processes while I watched the young men arguing and wrestling. "Brothers," said Elena, smiling. "And they fight all the time about something." She had used her hands and knocked her fists together to convey her message to me.

In the evening, we all sat on mats on the floor and sipped our cups of wine. I thought perhaps James and John were with Jesus the day I gave my last coins.

"I have heard the story before of how you fishermen ended up following a teacher all over the countryside, but Tabitha may be interested," said Simon.

"Our father Zebedee, and my brother James and me, and hired men had been fishing. The fish were small, and we kept a few. We were all sitting and mending our nets, same as the boat near us. Simon Peter and Andrew were tasked to mend their nets, and all of us were complaining." John paused and sipped wine.

"Jesus was there by the Sea of Galilee. A big crowd of people was gathered around him, and he was about forced to the water's edge, ya see. He stepped into the boat of Simon Peter, and they went out a ways. He was probably tired, ya see, so He sat down and taught people about God from the boat," James said.

"Jesus finished talking and wanted them to take the boat out to the deeper water and let down their nets. We had all fished throughout the night and had no fish to bring up. We decided to listen to him since he seemed wise."

"We went out again, and Father was awed, ya, his mouth agape, as our nets were all full to the top when we drew them up. I wish ya could have seen us. We had such a big catch our mended nets were strained to breaking as we pulled in enough fish to almost sink our boat. Jesus is a miracle worker, ya see."

"Father wanted him to fish with us, but instead Jesus asked James to come along with him. I turned to help Father when Jesus spoke to me. He said he wanted us to be his followers. I know this may sound strange, but he told us from now on he wanted us to fish for people. Immediately, we left our father and his hired men in the boat to follow Jesus. There is a lot more to tell about his teaching." John's face shone.

"Let me tell it. He's a teacher and the son of a

carpenter in Nazareth, but he really talks like he's God's own son. Ya got to believe, should ya see the magic." James' face was aglow and as he moved his hands to express his words, his long hair swayed.

"Not magic, miracles. Not simply where to fish like he did for us, but healing sick people and blind people. We have been following him and encouraging people to believe his words. It is like fishing for people."

"Ya have to wonder how Jesus is in a lot of trouble, and we have to hurry back. Officials are afraid Jesus will do away with them and rule over everyone. I fear for his life because those dogs are ruthless. He doesn't believe in violence, so I don't know how to protect Jesus, ya see."

"I think we can be mean enough to beat up those high and mighty Pharisees and Sadducees." John's kind face grew grim, and he balled up his fists.

James entertained us with another story. "Did ya ever hear about Elijah? He was a great prophet of old. The Lord Almighty told him to warn people about a drought. He did, and the Lord asked him to go to the *Wadi Cherith*. When he stayed there, ya, he had water at first from the wadi, and ravens brought him food so he did not starve." He paused to catch his breath, sip wine, and nodded at his brother.

"When the water dried up, the Lord told Elijah to go to Zarephath. He asked a widow for water and food. She gave him a drink but told him she had no bread, only a little meal and oil. She had planned to bake it into a cake for her son and herself, and when it was gone, she would let herself die," said John.

My heart raced as I found the tale he told seemed much like my life. When I gave my last coins to the Temple treasury, I was ready to go home and die.

"Ya, Elijah asked the widow to bake him a cake first and then bake some for herself and her son. He told her not to be scared. The Lord was with her, ya see. She trusted and built a fire to bake. There was enough meal, ya see, and oil not only for Elijah's bread, but also enough for them. Was she surprised! After that, the jar of meal was never empty, and the oil pot stayed full. Elijah had been sent from the Lord God of Israel."

"I believe a miracle has been done for me," I said.

"We were at the Temple the same day you put coins into the treasury, and Jesus told us you had given all you had to live on. You were blessed for your faith," John said.

"You saw me. Who blessed me? Was it the Lord whose name I cannot say, or Jesus?"

"The Lord blessed you."

I nodded my head but did not fully understand.

Simon stood and stretched his arms over his head. "The mats you boys slept on last time you were here are rolled up over there in the corner. You may sleep up on the roof if you like. I am going to go to bed and trust you will all do the same."

"Thank you for everything. We leave in the early morning," said John.

The next day, the cloth lay in front of me in a colorful array. Some smelled like flax or exotic spices. I enjoyed looking at the fabrics and feeling the textures with my fingertips. There was a fine ivory color linen piece I longed to turn into something beautiful. I wondered how it could have become part of my stack of cloth, as white linen was reserved for priestly garments or royalty. I imagined how elegant I would look wearing it, even though it was too rich for me. My reverie was broken when a woman came to the door begging. At her side was a small boy, with arms as thin as twigs, dressed in a tattered tunic he had outgrown.

Elena gave them some cheese and bread, and a cup of milk for the boy. The timid woman talked in a weak voice, and I realized she spoke my language. I came closer. The woman's cloak was ragged, and her tunic was no better. They were barefoot, and the boy's eyes, set deep in his face under dark up-turned brows, were sad lusterless brown pools.

"I would like to help you," I said.

She looked at me with probing eyes. "How?"

"Come in." Elena motioned for them to enter. The woman hesitated and then entered.

"See the cloth. I can sew and will make a garment for you and a tunic for your son." Excitement lifted my spirits as I thought this was the beginning of a new life for me. I looked into her dark, shiny eyes.

"I am Lois, and my son is Seth." She twisted her garment hem nervously and had tears in her eyes. "He needs clothing, but I cannot pay you to make anything, I am sorry."

"Oh, no, I do not ask any money. I have very little, but I can sew and I want to make something for you. The cloth was a gift. Please select the one you want."

"You choose," she said, wiping her eyes with the back of her hand. The boy stood at her side, unaccustomed to any attention.

"What color do you want?" I asked Seth.

He did not say anything but looked at his mother. When she nodded, he bent down and shyly touched a sturdy brown cotton fabric.

"A wise choice for you," I said. I saw Lois gazing longingly at the linen I had dreamed of using for my new tunic and hoped she would not select it. I looked at her, ready to give it up, but she only shook her head.

"You are too good, but thank you for making something for Seth."

I unfolded the fabric to its full length. I held an end of the brown cotton next to the boy to get an idea of his size for accurate cutting. "There is enough for a tunic for you and one for Seth. Would you like it?"

"I cannot take it." The woman bent her head and was overcome with emotion. "We must go." She turned to Elena to thank her for the food, took her son by the hand and slowly walked away.

"Come in a few days. I should be finished with his tunic." My elation soared as I had sewing to do.

Simon was delighted to hear what I was doing with

the cloth. "There are many poor people here, especially widows. Their husbands sail away and never return, often lost at sea, drowned, or attacked by pirates. It is sad. As neighbors, we try to do what we can to help, and we give them food."

"Where do they live?" I asked.

"Some live with each other out of necessity, and some may still have the house their husband provided while he was living. Others wander around with no place to lie down at night except the streets."

"I would like to go into the town and see what I can do."

Simon shook his head. "The poor have always been, and no doubt always will be. I do what I can and give boys a job kneading the skins in the trough. Sometimes an older child will try their hand at scraping hair from the hides. What more can one do?" He shrugged and lifted his hands.

"You and Elena are kind and caring. I am sure it helps when you give their children some work and pay them. I can sew these pieces of material I have into garments for those who need them."

"I am certain now you have done it for one, more people will come around. You do not need to go into town unless you want to."

"Thank you again for giving me the sack of cloth."

"The material is yours, and I thank you for the garment you made for Elena."

My days were peaceful, and I seldom smelled the

stench of leather-making. I had been with Simon and Elena for nine moons and felt at home. A man knocked on the door of Simon's house. When Simon opened the door, the man asked, "Is Meydl Tabitha here?"

"I am here," I called and trembled, seeing it was Samuel's servant at the door. I feared there could be a dire message.

Twenty-One

S heaf bowed. "They were not sure you would still be here."

"Is my daughter ill? How are Samuel and Lottie?" My life pulse was pounding.

He nodded. "All are well. My lord's wife bade me go in haste to accompany you home. Your daughter wants you to make wedding clothes."

"Oh, I am relieved. I have lost count of how much time passed since I left." The anxiety drained from me and excitement took its place. "Of course, I will come home to sew her dresses."

"I trust you will not leave until morning. I have not heard your name, young man," Simon said.

"Sheaf." He bowed, his dark hands lifted in greeting, and he smiled a crooked smile exposing a wide gap in his yellowed teeth.

"You are welcome to unroll the mat in the corner for your bed. I trust you saw the well on your way here."

"Thank you. I will make my bed outside." He bowed shyly and took the mat Simon offered.

Simon said, "You may make your bed on the roof as it is comfortable up there."

I was so excited, sleep eluded me. I did want to make my daughter's wedding clothing and be there for the preparations. I packed a few things, my sewing basket, and the lovely linen piece. I was happy I had not used it. While the sun was not yet risen, I began the trek home with Sheaf carrying my sack.

The sun had dropped away from the sky as we kept on. All was well. We walked apace and did not stop to sleep. I was overjoyed as I saw the familiar outline of my friend's house come into view in the moonlight.

"Welcome home. How was your trek?" Samuel asked. He had been expecting me and met us.

"It is great to be home again. It was pleasant weather. There was a cool breeze as we started from Joppa, but it faded away." Samuel gave me cheek kisses and walked with me. He thanked Sheaf, and let him go.

"Mother, mother," Marian rushed out the front door when she heard me. After we embraced and kissed, I saw Lottie.

"You are alive and well." Lottie had tears in her eyes as she had missed me. My eyes were moist as we clasped arms and kissed cheeks. "You must be starved. I have bread, cheese, and wine. Let us all celebrate. First I have a basin of water for your sore feet." Candles glowed and lit the room.

Marian knelt by the basin of water and bathed my feet. It felt soothing to rest them in the cool water. She dried them with a soft towel. Warm and happy, I basked in the love of my daughter and friends. We would like to have talked the whole night, sharing memories and what I was sewing in Joppa. Marian was full of details about her wedding. When she saw my eyes grow heavy, she said, "Mother, you are tired and need to lie down. We will talk again in the morning."

I drifted contentedly to sleep with the sound of a night bird calling outside and a gentle breeze wafting into the window above me. I wondered at my life and how it had turned around after I gave my last coins to the Lord. My daughter was marrying a good man. I had new friends in Joppa and sewing to do. I thanked the Lord for all his gifts to me, but I wondered how much he listened to me.

The next morning Marian was excited to give me details of what had taken place since I left. She had met with her future husband, Azel, three times in the company of Samuel and Lottie. Each time he had treated her with respect and had given her some new gift. "Look at the lovely necklace he gave me." She unwrapped a gold chain set with blue and green stones that formed a cascade of brilliance.

"Oh, he must be a generous man to give you such a fine gift."

"Here is a new embroidered scarf. He trades with Parthians and others when he travels to sell olive oil."

"Wonderful. He does make good olive oil. Your father used to have our olives pressed there."

"Did we have crops when I was small?" She looked at me with doubtful eyes.

"Yes, we did. I lost everything through drought, your Uncle Uzziah, taxation, and my own lack of knowledge. Thank YHWH for Lottie and Samuel who have loved and raised you. I am truly sorry I had nothing to give you."

"Mother, please do not despair. You have given me so much love, and you could not have entrusted my care to better parents. I love you and will be pleased you are making beautiful wedding garments for me."

"You know I love you, Marian. I have longed for this day and will enjoy sewing for you." I opened my bag and grasped the ivory linen. In one motion of my hands, I flared it out for her to see its luxurious texture.

"Oh, Mother." She clapped her hands. "The cloth is the finest I have seen."

"It is so lovely." Lottie came into the room as I was spreading the cloth.

"I think it is enough for the outer garment." I lifted the fabric to drape it around Marian.

"Fit for a queen." Lottie admired it.

"And our daughter." We clasped both our hands and touched foreheads.

I had designed her wedding attire in my mind, and I measured the length and the width of fabric on her. In my sewing basket, I had plain thread with which to sew and more colorful ones I would use to embroider her dress.

Marian watched with rapt attention as I began to cut, drape, and sew her wedding attire. The outer garment would be linen, and the undergirding tunic cotton material to complete the finished gown she would wear. My love for her went into every stitch I took. I had time to sew as the wedding was over two months away, yet my excitement over the beautiful dress I was creating compelled me to push on hour after hour.

"Mother, you must stop to drink water and eat." Marian brought a tray with bread, olive oil, cheese, and figs.

"Thank you, I forget meals and water when I have something as beautiful as this to make."

Lottie looked over my shoulder. "I do not know how you keep your stitches in such an even line. I cannot do it."

"I have practiced for years to create a fine garment like this, and I especially want to make it as perfect as possible for Marian. I have had some problems with my thread breaking." I shook my head and raised my eyebrows. "I hope to find unbreakable thread one day."

Lottie laughed. "Oh, there's no such thing as unbroken thread. Where did you get such a rich fabric? I bought a length of tan woolen and also white cotton material from a booth in Jerusalem, hoping you could use it." She held it up.

"Thank you, I can use them both, for she will have layers of garments. I have a sack of material Zeke left for Simon when he traded with him. His wife does not sew, and they gave it to me. I do not know how it came to be mine, except I believe the Lord is taking care of me so I can help others."

As the outer garment took shape, I placed it on Marian, and it fit her well. While I embroidered purple, red, and yellow flowers on the coat, sometimes by the light of an oil lamp, Marian and I talked. She said, "I have spent some days with Serena and have learned a lot about herbs and how they are used to treat illness. She has shown me how to pound and rub dry mint leaves into a fine powder to add to olive oil and use as a salve for sore backs or legs. I do like healing people but have only gone with her two times to care for one who was ill."

"Your grandmother is a midwife, and she will be proud you are interested in becoming a healer. I think you love it as much as I do sewing. Have you spoken with Azel about continuing your training?"

Marian was quiet. At last, she looked at me. "No, I have not asked him. I thought he might be more easily convinced when we are married. What do you think, Mother?"

"Are you afraid he will refuse?"

"Not fearful, but reluctant, because he could forbid it."

"So, you are putting off knowing if you might be

able to do something you have your heart set on. It is best to face it without delay and let him know how much you desire to do this. I believe he would respect you more than if you wait until you are wed to reveal it."

"What will I do if he will not let me learn to become a healer?" She had tears spilling down her rosy cheeks.

"Come here." I took my daughter into my arms and embraced her. "If you want to be a healer badly enough, you may have to choose."

"You mean, either give up marrying him or give up learning healing arts?" She sniffled and wiped her face on the sleeve of her tunic.

"Yes, you would have to decide what to do if he objects. Can you see why I believe you must tell him now?"

"I do, but it does not make it easy. When I see him at the appointed time, I will tell him. Can you be with me, please?"

"I will." I was apprehensive sitting with my daughter who was young and vulnerable. She was accustomed to being allowed to do things most girls could not do because Samuel and Lottie adored her and had given in to her wishes. Studying healing arts was one of their indulgences for her. Another was freedom to roam alone in the meadow and gather herbs once Lottie had pointed out the place they grew.

I had been busy sewing and visiting and had not gone to my hut but decided to stop for a while and go there. As I approached a certain spot on the trail, the memory of Uzziah crept into my mind. Sweat drenched my back and hands, and I ran the rest of the way to my door. When I opened it, I stood motionless, inhaling the stale odor of the hut. While I knew it was improbable, my life pulse quickened as I imagined him sitting inside waiting to attack me.

Twenty-Two

arian peered out to watch Azel approach with servants in a fine horse-drawn carriage. I looked at her anxious face and wondered if my child was ready for this man.

Samuel welcomed him into their home for the evening meal. "Come in, Azel. Let us have a cup of wine while we wait for the meal to be put on the table. The evening is fair, and we could enjoy sitting outside if you would like. How is the olive business going?"

"Business is good, and yes, I would like a drink out in the fresh air." Two cups of wine were poured before they went out.

Lottie, Mia, Marian, and I finished putting the sumptuous lamb stew on the table along with fresh baked bread. Lottie had placed a simple beige cloth on the table and set out plain ceramic bowls and carved wooden spoons. Marian had found some yellow and white flowers she put in a vase on the table. It was festive.

"Come inside before the stew cools," Lottie said.

Samuel and Azel sat at the head and foot of the table, Marian and I on one side. Lottie sat on the opposite side where she had access to the kitchen for anything she might ask Mia to replenish.

Candle glow warmed the table as Samuel asked a simple blessing on the meal. As we ate, I tried to think of something to say and waited for Samuel. He and Azel talked of crops and weather.

"This is a delicious stew," Azel said. He looked at Marian.

"Mia made it, but I am learning from her how to make stew and other dishes."

"I look with anticipation to have you grace my home, but you will not have to cook unless you wish to. You may supervise the slaves who do it."

"Then I will have time to do other things." Marian looked at me for support.

Lottie rose and went to the kitchen area to ask Mia to bring more stew. Samuel sopped the bottom of his bowl with a piece of bread. I smiled at Marian and nodded.

"Thank you," Azel said to Mia who had ladled stew into his empty bowl. "What kinds of things would you do?" Azel sounded earnest but had a twinkle in his eyes and a smile forming on his face not quite covered by his beard.

"I want to learn about healing. I was ill some months ago and went to Ekron to see Serena the healer. She let me pay for my care by working for her, and I decided I want to become a healer like her. Will you let me study with her?" Marian stopped speaking, her shining brown eyes turned to Azel to see the effect of her words. Her smile faded.

He had a startled expression on his face. "Today is the first time I have heard of any illness. Is she afflicted with some ongoing malady?" Azel spoke to Samuel, his brow wrinkled with concern.

"No, no, she is not sick," Lottie blurted, although he had asked Samuel.

"No, do not be concerned. It was a short problem, and Serena gave her medicine to bring about complete wellness." Samuel had put his hand on Azel's arm and looked earnestly at him. "Your bride is healthy."

"She looks well." Azel's shoulders relaxed, and he put a spoonful of stew in his mouth.

We were all silent except for thumps of spoons in our bowls as we finished our meal. Marian stared at her bowl and did not eat as she waited for Azel to answer.

"Do you think those rainclouds on the horizon will pour down and make working in our fields impossible?" Samuel tore off another chunk of bread as he spoke.

"It might. I must take my leave to be ahead of it."

The meal ended amicably, and Azel left to escape the oncoming storm.

After he had gone, and we were clearing dishes, Marian burst into tears. "I asked him, but I do not know if he truly heard what I said. He did not say anything to me, only to Samuel. Afterward, all the men could think about was the oncoming weather. Ooh! Do you think he is an unreasonable man?"

"Not an unreasonable man, a man. I believe he is good and fair, but we will see." I put my arm around her and let her cry. "His main concern was your health." I wondered if she was having doubts about marrying a man over twice her age.

In the morning, I continued sewing. I embellished Marian's cloak sleeves with embroidery of flowers, leaves, and vines. Absorbed in my work, I did not see Marian come watch me.

"Mother, I will be the best-dressed bride there ever was."

"You will marry him without an answer to your question about becoming a healer?"

"It would be late now to change my mind, even if my three parents allowed me to stop the betrothal. You have put so much work into my dress. Samuel would be embarrassed, think me ungrateful, and might never speak to me again."

I did not know what to say. I hoped she would be able to study healing arts as well as be married and raise a family. I completed sewing her wedding garments two weeks ahead of the ceremony. She did look lovely in them.

Since Azel's parents were deceased, Lottie helped him direct trusted servants to deliver the message to neighbors about the upcoming celebration. With Azel's kitchen slaves, we planned the meal. Large jars of wine were brought from storage, and preparation of honey cakes, bread, soft goat cheese, figs, dates, herbs, and spiced fruits filled the air with their aromas. One meal would include boiled eggs, a fertility symbol, and the oval shape symbolic of eternal life with no beginning or end. During the weeklong celebration, under the supervision of Samuel, the servants would roast Azel's chosen fatted calf. We were caught up in these plans with much joy. I wished Jacob was alive to share the excitement.

While I was involved in the activities, I tried not to think about what I would do after the wedding. I saw a little dust billowing as I sat outside with some mending. A man dismounted from his horse and said, "I have a message for Marian."

"Did I hear my name?" Marian came outside to see him. Her eyes grew wide in recognition, and a smile brightened her face as she saw the handsome young man and the black horse.

"Yes, Serena wants your help if you have the time. Her husband Philip has taken ill, and she has many patients in her care. She would be grateful if you can come."

"Right now? I am to marry soon." Marian looked at me with pleading eyes as she had when she was a child faced with a difficult choice. "And ye . . ."

"How many days do you suppose she will be needed?" I asked.

"As long as she likes, but I believe any time at all would be helpful. I must hurry back to run Philip's metal-working business while he is abed."

"I will go for a week. Wait while I pack a few things." Marian's face grew red with excitement.

"My name is Tabitha, and Marian is my daughter." I looked at the handsome young man with concern he had come alone to get her. I wondered why Philip had not sent a trusted slave.

"I am Obed, and I am happy to meet you. I thought Samuel and Lottie were her parents."

"They were her parents while I was away, but I am her mother. If she wants to go, shall I get someone to take her?"

"Marian is safe with me, and we can ride swiftly on my horse. I assure you she will return in time for her wedding."

"The well is over there. Give yourself and your horse some water and rest a few moments before you travel. Would you like something to eat?"

"I will drink from the well and water my horse, thank you. Yes, I would not mind a morsel of bread."

When Obed smiled, his tanned cheeks dimpled above a trimmed beard. He and the dark horse went trotting to the well. Marian was ready in a short time, and Mia came with a tray of bread and cheese. He rode up and nimbly alit from his horse.

"Thank you so much," he said. "I am glad to see Marian is well."

"We are all grateful. Take care of her on the ride to Serena, and see to it she is home safely within a week. She is to be married." Lottie had come out to watch them leave.

"She will be protected with me."

"Carry my greetings to Serena. I hope Phillip heals soon." Lottie waved.

"I will give them your good wishes." Obed clasped his hands together for Marian to step onto and mount the horse. She giggled and placed first one and then the other bare foot onto his hands. He lifted her up, got her settled, and quickly hopped astride in front of her and grabbed the reins. The horse galloped away, with Marian clasping her arms around Obed's waist.

"Where are your sandals?" I waved. An odd feeling of dread crossed my mind and I shuddered as I went inside. I got my sewing basket and continued mending a tunic. My thread broke. "Shall we visit Serena and see if we can be of help?" I asked Lottie.

"Oh, what might we be able to do? We are busy enough here with the details of a wedding." Lottie laughed to make light of it. She tasted the vegetable stew she had in the hearth kettle, wiped her brow with her sleeve, and looked at me with narrowed eyes. "You should stop worrying about Marian. How much did you concern yourself over her the past years when she was under my care?"

"I did not mean anything I said to be critical of you. And, yes, I was mindful of my daughter every day I was apart from her. You do not know how heart-wrenching it was to give her to you when I could no longer provide for her. Lottie . . ." I stopped trying to knot the broken thread. "You are my closest friend and you have done more for me and Marian than anyone else." Tears filled my eyes, unbidden. "I do not fault you in any way. She adores you and Samuel." I stood and went to her.

"You are concerned about the young man who whisked her away." Her voice softened.

"Yes. What do you know about Obed?"

"He works for Serena's husband in his metal business and is learning the trade from him. The young man is friendly to everyone. I am unsure of his upbringing as we can plainly see he cuts his hair and trims his beard in a different way than would a devout man, and he has pale brown eyes."

"He is a Gentile, then."

"I believe so, but I do not know from where." She lifted her hands.

"The servants say he is from afar." Mia was stirring the stew.

"I am clearly uneasy. Did you see the way he enjoyed cupping his hands for her bare foot as he helped her onto his horse?" I shook my head, concerned about Marian. I put my hand on Lottie's arm, and she patted it.

"Marian is a smart young woman. Obed is behaving as any young man would with a lovely girl." Lottie winked.

"It is what worries me."

When Samuel came home from the fields at dusk, and we sat at table he paused, looked from Lottie to me, asked, "Where is Marian? Has she taken ill?"

Lottie looked at me, and I at her, expecting each other to speak. Lottie said, "She has gone to help Serena for a few days as Philip has taken ill."

"The horseman I saw coming down our trail came for her?"

"Yes," Lottie said.

"And you women let her run off with Obed?"

"Oh, it was not running off. Philip is ill, and Serena needed her." Lottie looked at Samuel, handing him a pepper spice he liked to sprinkle into his stew.

"I do not like for her to go away with him. Why was I not consulted?" Samuel's angry voice shook the air.

"Serena has been good to her, and I thought Marian should be able to make up her own mind. She will soon be a married woman." Lottie spoke evenly.

"It is not right. Serena is half sorceress." His face grew red and his fists clenched.

"She healed Marian." Lottie looked evenly at Samuel.

"And what do you think of this?" He glared at me.

I did not know how to answer. I looked from Lottie to Samuel, feeling perplexed. "I am as concerned as you and think someone should go to Serena and make sure all is well. It was my first thought when I saw my daughter go ride away with a man I do not know."

"I will take off from my fieldwork and bring her home. She should not have gone."

"There is no need for you to. I will fetch my daughter."

"Mia has offered to go," said Lottie.

"No need for you to make the trek, Tabitha. Mia can come with me and stay if Serena needs help." Samuel shook his head and strode outside.

I had no further appetite for the food but sipped a cool spoonful of broth. Marian was my daughter, though they had been her parents for the past few years. "I want to go."

"No, I must do my fatherly duty. With either of you women, she will talk you into allowing her to stay there."

"You will not lay a hand on her," I said.

"Only if it becomes necessary." He raised a hand as a father ready to spank a child.

At first light the next morning, Samuel took a donkey he had purchased from a neighbor and agreed to let Mia come with him. He seemed in a more favorable mood, so I hoped he would treat Marian fairly.

In the evening Samuel came home with a tearful Marian loaded onto the donkey against her will. Mia had stayed to help Serena. Marian sulked, refused food, and would tell me nothing about the ordeal. She reclined on pillows on her mat.

The days were a blur of activity. Marian's horse ride

with Obed to Serena was not mentioned again until long after the wedding.

Twenty-Three

The wedding was a weeklong celebration of feasting. Stone jars of wine waited like silent servants beside the festive tables. Azel and Samuel had handpicked the fatted calf. Marian's dress was complete and fit her beautifully. I reflected on my own wedding day many years ago and missed Jacob more than ever. In my heart, I said, "Lord, bless my daughter and give her and Azel a good life with healthy children."

The canopy was set up in the courtyard of Azel's house. It was a clear evening and the stars were beginning to awaken, shining in the darkening blue heavens. Azel wanted the wedding to take place at dusk, as was his family tradition. God assured Abraham, "I will bless thee ... and multiply thy seed as the stars of heaven ..." The evening stars were a fulfillment of the holy words.

Marian was clothed and veiled in her dressing room. Azel, adorned in a white robe, was the first escorted to the chuppah by ten men who each carried a lighted candle symbolizing the Ten Commandments. Samuel, Lottie, and I walked around him three times, symbolically warding off any evil. Then we moved to the side of the canopy. Marian was escorted by bridesmaids all carrying candles. She walked around Azel three times and stood on his right side for the ceremony. The cantor touched her veil and chanted, "O sister! May you be the mother of thousands."

A thin ceramic cup was filled with wine for Marian and Azel, and they drank from it. The *ketubah*, spelling out the legal obligations of the husband, was read and signed by two neighbors as witnesses. Prayers were said after each sip until the wine was finished.

Tears welled in my eyes. I was overwhelmed by feelings of love, of loss, of hope and faith all rolled into one.

Azel handed Marian a gold coin. "Behold thou art consecrated to me forever with this coin." He put the wine cup on the ground, stomped, and smashed it.

The celebration was festive with many neighbors attending. Some brought tents to stay all week as we danced, ate, drank wine, and visited. We danced the *hora* with energy. As we whirled around and around, I felt lighthearted. Mother sat nearby, smiled at me and stood, waving a scarf in the air.

Naomi and her husband had brought Mother. I was excited to see her but grieved to see she was bent like a wilted flower and walked with the aid of a staff. I took her to my home to rest. She removed her yellow linen scarf and said, "Look at my hair, so thin and white you can count the number growing out of my pink skin."

"Mother, your hair tells a story of long years of loving and caring for us. Wear it proudly like a crown." I arranged extra cushions on the sleeping mat for her comfort.

"I do not think I wear it like a queen, but you are so kind." She smiled, showing gums where her teeth used to be as she settled in with a sigh.

"Your kindness and love made me who I am." I gave her a cup of water, as I knew she would not be able to chew the meat and fruit we had been given. "I have a soft vegetable soup for you to eat, if you would like."

"Yes, I would appreciate it. While I am tired, I have enjoyed the day."

As I brought her the soup, I said, "I am glad you are feeling strong enough to be here for this special occasion."

"I was pleased to see you made Marian's beautiful dress."

"Oh, yes. I enjoy sewing clothing more than anything else. Thank you for teaching me. I have a good work to do for needy people with my stitching skills."

While it was a little walk to my house, it was special to visit with her away from the crowd. Mother held me warmly before she went home with Naomi. "Daughter, I love you as dearly as if I had borne you."

Once they had all left, I did not want to remain in

my hut alone as it held many bad memories. I stayed with Lottie to relax a few days and then I headed to Joppa.

"Must you leave?" Lottie and I were sipping a calming herbal tea sweetened with honey.

"Yes, I have work to do in Joppa."

"I hope you are not stomping the hides to soften them in foul-smelling slop."

I laughed. "No, not at all. Right now, I am living with Elena and Simon, but I plan to find a place in the town. Sewing keeps me occupied. I have sewn some tunics and a cloak for people. Orphans and widows are in need."

"If you give the garments away, how will you live? I think you ought to ask payment for things you make."

I looked at my friend and hoped she could understand. "They are poor and cannot pay. The Lord will provide." Most of the time I was confident of my faith, but doubts assailed me in the night when sleep would not come. "You are such a good friend, and I do not know how I would have taken care of Marian without you."

"You know I loved having Marian with me. It was so good of Naomi to bring your mother to the wedding. She is frail. Is she doing alright?"

"I am thankful Naomi cares for her. There is always someone who needs help in life. I suppose we are all in the places we need to be."

"You have faith. I try, but so many times I doubt.

After all, the Lord did not bless me with my own children." Lottie was tearful. "With Marian gone, my house is as good as empty."

I was not sure about my faith but did not dispute her words. I went to her and we embraced. We were interrupted by loud, angry voices. We looked up anxiously and went to the door to peer outside.

Obed brought Mia home. She got down from the horse and walked toward the house while Obed hurried to the well. Samuel raised his fists at Obed who watered his horse at the trough. "I told you not to come to this place again."

"A man has a right to go anywhere he pleases, and you cannot stop me."

"You took our daughter without asking me." Samuel grabbed Obed by the front of his tunic.

"She rode the horse with me, nothing more, old goat!"

"Be gone, and do not return." Samuel let go of him with a shove.

Obed mounted and galloped away spewing grains of rock and sand.

Mia came into the house.

"Lottie?" I was perplexed because Samuel seldom raised his voice. While I was not concerned for Mia, I wondered if anything unseemly had happened to my daughter.

"Samuel is overly protective of Marian and does not trust Obed. He believes he should have been consulted before Marian went with the boy to help Serena."

"Did he have words with Serena and Philip or only Obed?"

"Obed. He was afraid the young man had taken advantage of Marian."

I went nearer Lottie and touched her arm with affection. "Samuel should not have to worry about her anymore as she is married and secure." I felt torn, yet eager to be on my way.

Lottie looked into my eyes and returned the touch. She lifted her eyes to the heavens and shook her head.

"I hate to leave, but I feel I must." We embraced.

"Please stay, as I will miss you." Lottie held my arm as if to keep me there. We shared the moment.

I left very early in the morning before Samuel and Lottie could object. I had not gone far when I saw Sheaf trailing behind me. He gave me his gap-toothed smile and caught up to take my pack. The sun appeared from behind puffy clouds and warmed my walk. I was elated heading to Joppa, and my steps were light. Nothing gave me any pause as I trekked, and I was surprised when I was close to my destination as the sun had dipped low in the sky and disappeared. Yet as I approached the seaside and smelled the air, doubts assailed me. Should I have stayed with Lottie, or in my own house nearer Marian?

Twenty-Four

S imon was working as I came near. He waved with his scraping shell in his hand. "We have missed you. How was the wedding?"

"I missed you too. My daughter's marriage to Azel was a happy affair, and she is secure with him. You are busy at work, and I am eager to go see Elena."

"I must stop as it is now dark, so I will be there to visit and sup. She will be glad you are here."

We kissed cheeks when Elena met me at the door. "You must tell me everything. How did your daughter look in the beautiful garment you made?"

"Thank you. There is much I want to say, but I am very tired and will describe it all tomorrow."

"Your walk went well?"

"Yes, it did." I smiled. Elena was speaking Aramaic. Simon had been teaching her while I was away.

When Simon came home and we sat to eat, he had little to say. I thought he was weary. "Have you heard what happened to the teacher in Jerusalem?"

"No, I have not," I said.

"They crucified him." He coughed and cleared his throat. "I cannot believe the cruelty of the Roman way to kill criminals. The Sanhedrin condemned him, and Pilate tried and convicted him." He shook his head. "I am in deep sorrow for him and all his followers."

I sat trying to make sense of what he said. "Who? Surely not the rabbi Jesus. I feel so sad for you and his friends."

"Yes, you met two of his disciples who stayed here and supped with us. He was a good man and spoke the truth. Which is why the authorities hated him."

Tears welled in my eyes as if Jesus had been a good friend I had known.

"More than a teacher, I believe he was a prophet of the Lord of Heaven. Some say he was Elijah. I doubt it, because why would he not present himself as such?" Simon shook his head.

Grief prevailed as we finished our meal in silence. I could not understand how something unjust and terrible could have happened to a good man. Elena and I cleared the table. She turned to me and grasped both my arms at the elbow. "I am happy you are here."

"So am I." I smiled and kissed her cheeks. "We will visit in the morning." I slept soundly.

Word spread around town Simon had a seamstress staying with him. Besides making Elena's dress, I had more sewing to do. People wanted garments, and my hands were seldom idle. One day a stately woman came. Simon introduced her, "Meet Esther, benefactor of the poor, one of the kindest women." She and Elena kissed cheeks, and Esther and I did the same.

Her scent was spring flowers, and I was awed at her attire of tan linen and colorful silk scarves.

She touched my arm and said, "Tabitha, I have heard much about your work and seen examples of your sewing expertise. I am here to beg of you to come to Joppa and live so your customers do not have to come all this way. I have a place for you to dwell and do hope it will be to your satisfaction." Esther pressed a small spiced-cloth to her nose to ward off odors of Simon's leather making.

"None of my customers have complained about the walk from town, and some say they enjoy it. You are kind to offer a place for me in Joppa, but I have no money to pay for it."

"At first you can sew for me to pay for your home."

"I need to buy cloth, of course, to make fine cloaks, tunics or whatever you wish." I said. My whole being was bouncing inside with excitement at the possibility of a home.

She nodded to Simon and Elena. "I would like to take Tabitha with me and show her the home she will have in Joppa. If it is to her liking, she may stay the night and we will send for her belongings later."

Elena packed a few food items for me and bade me go and enjoy, but to come visit soon. Although I was apprehensive, I gathered a small sack of things before we left. "I have never lived in a town," I said, as we walked past Simon, who waved.

"You are in for a new experience." She picked up a snail shell, held it up to show me the rainbow colors inside, and dropped it onto the sand.

"I like the pretty shell. I have not seen them before coming here. What is the town like?"

"Joppa has mostly mariners and families who have fished or dealt with foreign merchants and traders for generations. We have a number of widows, as sailors get lost in the Great Sea and beyond."

"Sad for them. I hope I can find a way for my sewing to help."

"You will." We walked past a boat dock. Muscular men, burned dark by the sun, were unloading cargo. One man stood idly watching. They were laughing and talking in different languages as they worked. Some were singing. "Do not look at the men, as they take it as an invitation," Esther warned.

I stopped abruptly, unable to move. I thought I saw a ghost among the men. My face became flushed with my life pulse pounding.

"Is something wrong?" She looked at me, concerned. "You seem afraid. I did not mean to frighten you."

"It was not your warning, but I thought I saw a man I supposed was dead."

"What man?" Her eyes were kind, yet probing.

"Uzziah."

Twenty-Five

After he had taken Silas back to his father, Uzziah kept walking through the vineyard where the small, purple grapes shriveled like many tiny babies unborn. He picked one, put it into his mouth, and made a face. "Hah, do you not want a son? I was supposed to stand in for you, Jacob, but your wife was as cold and dry as an old she goat." He spoke as though his brother lingered out of sight behind a vine. His full water flask flopped as he walked, the only sound besides his footsteps. He kept going, sometimes on the trail, yet he wandered off as one who has no destination.

On the trail, he found the dry creek. Trees provided shade and small patches of green plants thrived in the shade-dappled places. He remembered leaves Wills and Silas had plucked up as they traveled and sampled some green herbs as he was hungry. He was not in a hurry and rested frequently because he was not sure where he was going. He thought the Great Sea was in the general direction he traveled. When it became dark, he lay on a small patch of dry grass and leaves to sleep. He kept wandering on, not in a hurry to go anywhere.

When Uzziah approached Joppa, he saw the walled city. In the morning, he ventured onward to the seashore and saw fishermen mending nets. Boats had set out, and he could see several of them bobbing up and down as the men plied their oars. Farther along there were more boats, some larger for taking people and goods across the sea to other lands. A wooden dock was laden with all manner of items for trade. He went to watch the men loading and unloading cargo. Larger boats were tied there.

The fresh air was brisk and filled with fish odor. Men called to each other with bantering friendship, some in languages he did not know. A sense of wellbeing filled him as if he were safe at home. He stopped to give it some thought but could not discern why he should be at ease in a strange place. He approached two men who were holding a net they were inspecting. "Good day to you," Uzziah said. "How is the fishing?"

"Yesterday our nets were not heavy," the young man said. "We are going out to fish again today."

"Who taught you to fish?" Uzziah asked.

"I did," said the old man. "My name is Japho."

"I am Uzziah."

"You come from Judah by the look of you," he said.

"From the country where we grow barley crops,

grapes, and olives."

Japho turned his attention to the net and spoke to his son. The young man said, "I have fished with my father since I was a little boy. We must leave now." He waved his hand and grabbed an oar.

A one-armed man nearby struggled with a net he mended, and Uzziah stepped into the water beside his boat. Uzziah asked, "May I help?"

"Thank you. I manage by myself. You are not from these parts. Do you fish?"

"I have fished some in the Jordan using a net. Yet I would like to learn more."

"I am Daniel. Thank you. I could use some help. What shall I call you?"

"Uzziah. I will be glad to assist with the net and fishing."

"Waters will be bumpy as we go farther out. Take the oar and dip it into the sea to move us out. Can you do it?" Daniel showed him how to handle the oar with one arm.

"Yes, I will." Uzziah took the oar. In spite of no prior rowing experience, it felt natural.

Few words were spoken between them. Daniel was capable. The Great Sea lay before them, deep, dark blue, and shiny. It slapped at the boat with glee. Uzziah became soaked when a wave lifted it, then dropped them in a trough. "How can one fish in this sea?"

"Not yet," said Daniel. "Soon we will make it to a quieter place and let down our net. Did you see the flash of silver scales?"

"It was large." He tried to stay calm, but Uzziah found he could not stomach the bobbing up and down. So much for feeling at home, he thought. He emptied the meager contents of his stomach over the side of the boat and shook his head. Without a word, Daniel handed him a slice of ginger to chew and watched his reaction with a slight smile. "Thank you, a little sharp to taste, but my stomach has settled with it."

His confidence in his ability to handle the job grew. He rowed until Daniel grabbed an oar and pointed to a cove where they went to fish. They put down the anchor, a rock tied with a rope. Daniel handed him one end of the net and they cast it on the water.

"Thank you, much easier cast with another set of hands." Daniel settled on the bench in the boat.

"Have you always gone out in the boat alone?" Uzziah waited for Daniel to answer. He had been accustomed to Wills and knew when to say no more.

"No." Daniel's eyes looked to the horizon. "I think we will have a fine catch here. I see the signs. Caleb taught me how to read the sea and the fish."

"He was a good friend, then."

"Older brother."

"I had an older brother who died," Uzziah blurted and sucked in the sea air.

"Sad. My brother is gone." Daniel looked toward the sea. The slap, slap of waves filled the silence. "Time to haul in the net," Daniel said. It was a meager catch they deposited into the boat. They moved forward until they saw the banks and tree-lined coast close to them. Once again, the expert furl of the net went out, and this time it became heavy with all manner of fish as they moved with a current in the calm water.

When the net was drawn up, Daniel sorted fish by size and kind and strung them in groups. Uzziah rowed to Joppa. Men were selling fish when they came to the dock. Daniel sold his fish but saved a few to bring home to his wife.

"Uzziah, I appreciate your work." Daniel gave him some coins as payment.

"Will you be my guest for our evening meal, or would you prefer to have some fish to cook?"

"You are kind to ask me to come to your home. Yes, I will enjoy having sup with you and your family."

Daniel nodded his head. They finished cleaning the boat and carried fish home to prepare. As they walked, Daniel asked, "Where do you stay?"

"I came to Joppa this morning, so I must find a place."

"Stay with me and my wife. We have enough room. Will you rise early and fish with me?"

He fished with Daniel and was surprised at how easy it became to do what was needed. Perhaps fishing was in his blood as his mother had told him of her family's fishing history. He did not want to think about his past and tried to forget his life with Meydl Tabitha. One day as they returned home, Uzziah became wide-eyed and turned his head toward the market they passed. Two women were shopping, and one of them could have been her. Uzziah saw the woman who looked like Jacob's wife, now his wife, and watched her turn onto a path. Daniel went down the same way to go to his house, so they followed at a distance.

"You are attracted to those women," Daniel said, with a lighthearted tone to his voice. "One is older and richly dressed, and I believe her name is Esther. Some widows live nearby if you are interested."

"Perhaps." He had seen which house they entered. He carried the string of fish from which Daniel's wife Mary would make their meal. She greeted them with a warm rosy face, matched by the fire on the hearth where a globular-shaped pot raised promising aromas of vegetable soup. While she cooked, Daniel pointed to the loft in which Uzziah could sleep. The food smelled sumptuous, and his stomach growled insistently.

"Where did you eat on your travels?" Daniel asked.

"I ate herbs and berries on the trail here, and your food smells delicious." Uzziah said.

"Mary is a good cook." The men washed the fishy muck from their hands in a bucket of water before they sat to eat.

When he had finished eating, Uzziah took the leather pail Daniel gave him. "Thank you. I want to go to the well and then into the town."

"We fish early, so do not be out too late," Daniel said, grinning.

Uzziah filled the bucket and washed. It felt good to get several days grime cleaned from his body. The moon was out so he could see to walk. He passed the house where he had seen the women enter earlier. He wondered if they both lived there. His curiosity got the better of him and he pounded on the door a couple of times. Fists clenched, he wanted to break the door, and see the look on her face.

Twenty-Six

E sther frowned a little, yet smiled. "He is someone you know?"

"My husband, but I am sure it was someone who looked like him, as I believe he died at the hands of a wild animal who dragged him away a few years ago."

"I can understand your sudden fright. Are you feeling alright? We will make tea when we get to your home."

We came to a cleanly swept street lined with houses. Children played a running game and squealed with glee. We stopped in front of a small rock house with an upper room. A flat roof on top of the house and an outdoor stone stairway made it easy for someone to climb and look far to the sea. "This is the place I have for you. I hope you will like it." She opened the sturdy wood and metal door.

"The whole home to myself?" As I stepped inside, I saw the dirt floor in the large room was immaculate. A stone hearth and a wall of shelves in the kitchen area and a nice wood table with two benches were there. "It is wonderful. The table will be perfect for cutting out the garments I sew." I could not believe my good fortune. I was content, delighted. High windows let in air and sunlight, brick and wood plank stairs led to an upper room.

Esther lit the hearth and found a kettle to boil water for tea.

Fresh water and tea leaves were waiting for us, and I was overwhelmed by her thoughtfulness. I lowered my voice and looked up at her. "I will never be able to repay you."

"You will sew for me, and it will be enough." She smiled graciously. "After tea, we need to get you a bed and a few things for the night."

"I do not know how to thank you enough," I said. We sat on benches at the wood table to have tea. "So many things made of wood is a luxury."

"You do not have to thank me, as the Lord has been good to me, and I can share with others. As for the wood, much of it comes to us on sailing vessels, bringing it from forests far away."

On the market street, Esther bought two medium-sized green and brown rugs, a soft wool sleeping mat and a tan blanket. "We will not be able to carry it all," I said.

"Do not concern yourself." She hired a man with a cart and donkey to take the things and deliver them to my house.

After she made sure I was comfortable, she said, "You need not go to Simon and Elena tonight unless you wish, as I will send a runner to tell them. We can go visit them tomorrow to gather anything you have left there, or I can send someone to fetch them. There are dried fruits in the brown crock. Do you have enough food for tonight?"

"Yes, I have some cheese and bread in my bag, but I need to go to Simon for my sack of cloth and sewing supplies."

"I will go with you in the morning," Esther said as she left.

I was too tired and excited to eat, but had a little watered wine, figs, and bread before blissfully collapsing on my soft bed. Thankful and overwhelmed with everything, my eyes were shut but sleep would not come. The man who resembled Uzziah kept appearing in my head. Had he managed to survive, and now lived a different life? If so, I was not guilty of murder. I tried to forget him and all the pain. To clear my mind, I propped up on elbows and thought about the travels I had made with Zeke. I could visualize the scene below I had been overwhelmed with when I stood on the mountain heights. It was helpful to me to set my thoughts on pleasant times when I wanted to calm myself. I was being lulled to sleep when there was a loud knock on my door.

I stood, motionless. No one called a greeting. My usual habit of getting up to welcome travelers was not good in this strange place. If it was Uzziah, had he seen me? It could be someone who would rob and hurt me. I was afraid and flopped onto my bed. My life pulse drummed wildly as the pounding on my door was insistent. I trembled, cowered under bed covers.

I waited and looked around for some implement with which to defend myself. I did not call out or go to the door. My arms were prickly and my whole body wet with perspiration as I wondered if I should find a place to hide. What if he broke the lock? I lay there and worried about the fate awaiting me.

While I feared I would continue to be bothered, no more knocks came. I slept fitfully, hoping the person would not enter forcefully. I awakened to clouds in the morning. I tried to put dead Uzziah out of my mind, forget my anxious thoughts, and look forward to meeting new friends.

An overcast day greeted me when I felt bold enough to open my door. Nearby stood a poorly dressed woman who had two small girls clinging to her skirt. Her small hands could not have had the energy to knock forcefully last night. Her head was draped in a worn brown scarf. When she looked at me with hollow dark eyes my heart went out to her. She looked hungry. Elena had given me bread, cheese, and dried fruits when I left. I pulled apart some bread and smeared soft cheese onto it.

"Bless you for kindness," she said and gave each of her children pieces of the bread, and then put the last small morsel into her mouth. I gave her more bread.

"I see your children are in need of tunics. I have cloth. Let me sew them clothes."

"No." She shook her head and turned to go.

I called after her. "Come see me again."

She smiled and waved.

I had hardly closed the door when Esther came. "How was your first night?"

"Oh, Esther, there was a loud knock on my door. In the country, we welcome travelers into our homes no matter the time of day or night, but I was afraid to see who it was."

"Dear, dear Tabitha, you were right not to open the door. It could be dangerous for you. Sometimes it is a man who had too much strong drink and lost his way home. He keeps on knocking, thinks his wife has barred the door and will not let him in. Otherwise, someone may try to rob you or worse. Never answer after dark. I am so sorry it happened to you on your first night. We will look for a companion for you in the house. I was thinking of one of the widows."

"I would like to share the house with someone." I tried to sound grateful in spite of my apprehension.

"Surely I can arrange for you to meet the woman I have in mind. Today, I want to show you the whole marketplace in town."

She handed me a large woven sack and we strolled

down the street with our bags dangling from our arms. Despite clouds, sunshine peeked out for warmth. The booths and shops were laden with clothing, rugs, pottery, and all manner of household items.

"I need to go to Elena and Simon's place to collect my cloth and a few items," I said.

"I hope you do not mind, but I have taken it upon myself to ask someone to get your belongings and deliver them to you. When you go to visit, you will not have the burden of carrying things."

"Thank you." I was grateful for her thoughtfulness and generosity, yet I wanted to go see Elena.

The sea air mingled with many aromas of spices, fish, human sweat, and animal dung. Birds flew overhead, searching for a dropped morsel. Two floated down and squawked over one dropped crumb. We went to the food booths laden with orange and yellow carrots, dried lentils, green and purple leaves, and herbs tied in bundles. Smiling at the bountiful supply, I bought some herbs and vegetables and put them in my sack.

A fisherman was selling his catch nearby. He held one up as he saw me, "Fresh catch! I give a good price. How much will you offer?" I was unaccustomed to bargaining for food but answered with what I thought would reward him for his work. He responded, "Enough." I got the fish for supper. Happiness filled me as I was among people and buying my food, not depending on others. Esther bought two lengths of bright fabrics for her tunics. We tired after a while, and

I went home.

When we arrived, the cart with my sack of fabric and the rest of my supplies was waiting for me. Before it grew dark, I cut out a tunic for Esther from the fine orange material. Lois, the widow who had come to Elena with the small boy, came to my door. I asked her to come in and offered her tea to drink.

"I heard you were here. Thank you so much for making clothes for us. My son Seth is playing with his cousins. My sister is also a widow with children. Our husbands died at sea, and we have been living together since then. There are other widows living near us. We help each other and share what little we have. I am grateful for people like Simon who pay boys to work and Esther who finds homes for widows who have no shelter."

"There is no need to thank me. I am rewarded every time I pick up a needle and thread to make garments. Are there others who need clothing?" My heart soared like a bird in flight as I reflected on what the Lord had done for me. Sewing was work I could do well.

"I would like for you to sup with us tomorrow evening, and you can meet them."

"Thank you," I said. When she left, I closed the door and cooked my fish and herbs, feeling content.

The next day, I walked a short way down the street from my house to the home in which the group of widows lived. I kept my eyes on shadowed places one could hide, lest someone spring out unexpectedly. All was quiet, and a couple of people I met nodded as they went past. When I approached the widow's home, I saw a neatly swept entry with a small covered front porch. The hum of conversation echoed from a window. On the doorframe was a mezuzah I touched.

Lois answered my knock. "Wonderful you could be here, Tabitha. Come meet the others."

Four women sat on floor mats, and all but one rose as Lois brought me in. "Tabitha, this is Edna, Delia, Sarah, and Bithiah, the one who cannot stand."

"I am happy to meet all of you. I am a widow, too, and live a short way from here."

"Lois showed us the clothing you made for her and her son. It was kind of you," said Bithiah, whose wrinkled face grinned toothless at me from her mat.

"I do enjoy making things, and I hope you will let me sew a garment for you."

"My robe will do for a while, but when the wind blows cold, it reaches into the tattered places. I do not expect anything from anyone, and I try to provide for myself." Bithiah lifted her arm to show her threadbare sleeve.

"We all do what we can for each other," said Edna. She was a small woman with delicate features and long black hair.

"It is true for all of our friends. Will you have some bread and watered wine with us?" Lois said. She turned toward the group and smiled. "I must warn you, these friends will talk at length if you have a listening ear."

We ate and drank companionably. They were the wives of sailors or fishermen who had been lost at sea in a storm or other disaster. The most intriguing sad tale of all was from Delia.

"My husband Caleb was strong and capable. He had a thriving fishing business and slaves working for him. He went out every day even though he could have sent his brother, his trusted hireling, and his slaves, but he wanted to be out on the water. He told me he was more at home on the sea than he was on land. He always came in despite some of the most punishing gales you have ever seen. He came home to me every night, and I trusted he would always do so. One day he told me he might lay at sea overnight, but I should not worry. He wanted to go farther out than usual because he had heard of an area where the fish were plentiful." She sipped from her cup of watered wine and had a faraway look in her eyes as she continued.

"I spent an anxious night worrying about him, but when I awakened and saw the clouds move away to reveal the sun, I made ready for him to return. I washed and combed my hair. I put on a fish stew, made bread, and went to the pier to look for incoming boats. Many returned and I asked if they had seen Caleb. Not even his younger brother Daniel had seen him. I have been sorely vexed the two no longer fished together. Daniel blamed Caleb for the accident by which he lost an arm. I returned home to check on the stew as it simmered, savory with spices and fresh herbs."

"We have heard the story," said Bithiah. Her weary voice whined from listening to repeated renditions of the sad saga.

"Please go on if you can," I said.

"I returned to the pier and his boat was there, but floating free. I looked around, hoping to see his slave or hireling, but they were not there. I asked some fishermen who had straggled in if they had seen Caleb. One man observed the boat was there and not tied, so he secured it. No one had seen him, but they were not alarmed the boat had appeared. I walked the streets hoping to see him. Maybe he had been hurt, dazed, and did not know his whereabouts. But, no, I could not find him." She started to sob. "It was two years ago, so I suppose I am a widow. No one knows."

I went to her and put my arms around her. I remembered how unsettled I was when I did not know whether Uzziah was alive or dead. Although his death and disappearance was a mystery, I feared he might be alive.

This would be the first of many visits with the widows. The next time I came, I had made a tunic for Delia and a new robe for Bithiah.

"Oh, it is beautiful, and I will try it on so you can see it fits," said Delia.

"You should not have done it." Bithiah shook her head but put on her new tan robe. A smile creased her old cheeks and eyes, making her look years younger.

The other women clustered around as Delia and

Bithiah showed off their new clothing. I could see the longing in their eyes and made a measure of each one so I could sew garments for them.

Young Sarah, dark circles beneath her eyes, sat with me. I thought she might not be sleeping well. "Sarah, how long have you been widowed?"

A strange look crossed her face, and I wondered if she was a widow, or had escaped from a bad husband.

"About a year," she whispered and ducked her head.

Bithiah, ever the talkative one, said, "She is with child."

"Have you other children?"

"No." Her face became ashen, and I was glad she was seated.

Edna brought her a cup of water, and she seemed to brighten.

"We all help one another," Delia said. "Bithiah has been widowed ten years, Lois five, Edna four, and Sarah the least. I have been a widow for two years."

"I was widowed by my first husband, and his brother became my husband. My brother-in-law husband has been dead for a few years." My voice quavered from fear, but they probably thought it was grief.

"Would you like to have fish for supper? One of Caleb's friends brings us fish when he comes in if he has a large catch. The greens seller gave me some root vegetables left from last week. We are out of meal to make bread. I have oil."

"I will bring us some meal," I said and went to buy

it. I was surprised when Sarah came with me.

"What shall I do?" Sarah asked. "I am with child, but I think it is not from my lost husband. I was careless, and a man took me in the shadows one night. I feel ashamed. I have not told the others what happened to me."

I smiled kindly at her, but wondered at her confidence in me, since we had met today. I said, "My mother was a midwife so I learned about such things. You need to take care of yourself and be ready to care for the child. Be especially mindful you do not trip and fall. If you need someone to talk with, I will listen. I am a bit older, and my daughter Marian is nearly your age."

"Thank you, I would like to be your friend."

"I want you to be my friend too. Are your parents nearby?"

"My father was lost at sea many years ago when I was small, and my mother died when I was twelve."

"She had selected your husband before she died?"

"No, Matthias and I fell in love, and I became his wife. His father was Greek and part Roman, but his mother was a Jewess."

"How did you meet?"

"I was on the street selling sweet bread for a baker who was lame. Matthias bought bread and spoke with me, sometimes gave me fish and extra money. One day he asked me to be his wife."

"How sad he is gone."

"You are kind and good, Tabitha. Do you follow the

teachings of Jesus?" Sarah said. "It is all new, and I have heard few stories."

"I heard he was crucified. I do not know how I could follow his teachings or him."

"He is more powerful now. He was raised from the dead, and his disciples say it is true. I believe it." Her face shone with an inner joy as if candles lighted her pale brown eyes.

"I met disciples James and John at Simon the Tanner's house when I stayed there for a time. They told of miracles."

"The disciples are devout and tell how Jesus died for everyone and rose again from the dead. He went to heaven to be with the Lord."

"I have said silent prayers when I wanted to sort out things happening to me. I do not know if the Lord hears a woman's petitions."

"Believe in his son. He does listen. Please join all of us in prayers and telling people you meet about Jesus."

"How can I tell people about someone I did not know? What must I do?"

"Nothing, but simply tell everyone Jesus lived, died, and was raised. Keep on living like you do helping others."

"You have a good faith," I said. I did not know what to say as I pondered her beliefs but put it out of my mind. We were quiet for a time, and I asked, "Would you like for me to sew a new robe for you?"

"Oh, I would like it very much," she said.

I began sewing a new robe for her, and she stayed with me the rest of the day. I was glad for her company, and we became close friends.

I asked her to stay with me. In the next months, I continued to sew garments for widows and their families. I missed Elena and wondered how she fared, so I went to visit them.

"Tabitha, I am joyous to see you! Have you been well in Joppa?" We embraced and kissed cheeks.

"Oh, Elena, it is wonderful to be with you. I have missed our visits and will not take a long time before I return."

"What have you been doing?"

"I have been sewing clothing for the widows. Some live in a house together and share everything. I have a young woman staying with me who is expecting a child. It is good, and I help widows by making their garments. I believe it is what I was called to do. What is new here?"

Simon came in. "Well, well, look who is here. Happy to see you, but I must wash before I touch anyone." Simon gave cheek kisses after he washed.

"What is new here? I hope the leather business is thriving," I said.

"Business is good. Nothing new, but have you heard about Jesus? They say he rose from the tomb after he was crucified."

"My new friends talk of the same resurrection, but I cannot believe a man rose from the dead. Is he walking around for all to see?"

"I do not know." Simon said, "I heard they found his tomb empty, and a man who looked like Jesus appeared among people. Tabitha, we have been wondering how you are doing, but I fail to have time to go see you."

"Yes, I thought it was time I came to tell you I am well. You were busy when I went past today, so I did not stop to see you."

"And you are enjoying stitching?"

"Yes, I am."

"Let us have a drink and some of Elena's sweet treat."

"Oh, I would love it." Elena made the most delicious dessert consisting of thin layers of dough with honey in between them. It reminded me of chewing on a honeycomb. She had the cups of red wine poured and was cutting generous pieces of the dessert.

We were in the midst of enjoying the treat and conversation when we heard the swishing thuds of a horse galloping on the sand. We stepped outside. I was surprised, yet fearful, to see it was Obed, the man who worked for Serena's husband.

He dismounted and strode toward us. Simon greeted him, "Obed, good to see you, what brings you here? Come in and enjoy a sweet treat and some tea."

"Thanks for the treat, yes. I have not come for myself. I would like to speak with Marian's mother as I hoped she might be here."

Chills ran down my spine as I wondered if something had happened to Marian. I said, "What is it? Is Marian ill?"

"No, Serena sent me to tell you something is about to happen."

Twenty-Seven

bed settled on a mat to eat. "I did not see Marian, but she is about to birth a child and needs you," he said.

Elena and Simon assured me they would send word to my friends in Joppa, so they would not worry about me.

Obed sat on his black horse with me behind him, and we traveled fast. It was dark as we approached Serena's home. It appeared no different, yet I dreaded what I would find inside.

A pale-faced Marian was lying on a bed raised so Serena could tend her without stooping. Serena met me, kissed my cheeks, and spoke in hushed tones. "I am glad you came. Marian may give birth early, and as happens sometimes, the infant may not survive."

I nodded, smiled. "Obed said she needed me." I was delighted, yet worried. As I counted the moons since her wedding to Azel, I could not think how she was bearing a child this soon. I recalled Samuel's concern about her and Obed, but quickly put it out of my mind. Perhaps it had been longer since the wedding. I had lost all sense of time in Joppa sewing for the widows.

"How is my sweet Marian?"

Serena said, "Better now you are here, I am sure."

"Mother, oh I cannot say how much I want you here." Her hands reached toward me and tears glistened her eyes. "Thank you for summoning her, Serena."

"Are you in much pain?" I embraced her and sat on a stool beside her bed.

"Only as my belly grows hard, and then it softens and my pain eases some. Serena says it will be this way and harder until my baby is birthed."

"I will give you time for a visit since I have much work to catch up on." Serena took a close look at Marian, kissed cheeks with us, and left the room.

"I feel bad for you having such a difficult childbearing time. I came to be with you." I bent down and kissed her forehead, wished I could take away her pain.

"Thank you. I need you more than anyone. There is something I must tell you, but I do not know how." Tears welled in her eyes and spilled onto her cheeks.

"You know you can tell me anything, and I will listen." I put my hand on her arm. Her face was puffed and her feet out of the covers showed swollen ankles. The flickering lamplight caused shadows to emphasize the situation. She was suffering physically, but there was something else troubling her.

"Tell me what is on your mind." I stroked Marian's brow, smoothing her hair. "Are you getting along with Azel?"

"Yes, he is the kindest man and asks little of me. He is always inquiring if I need or want anything. He smiles and tells me he will give me everything in his power to provide." She began to cry. "I do not know how to tell him."

"What is it you want to tell Azel?"

"The child I carry may not be his."

I could not say anything. My throat tightened when I realized what she had said. It was no wonder she had called me and not Lottie and Samuel. Of course, I had no easy answer for her. I do not know how long I sat there thinking and not speaking. "Has Azel not consummated the marriage?"

"Yes, we did, but it was not right away as I had hoped. He was kind and thought to give me a week to adjust to being with him. Oh, I should have seduced him, made him come to me, but I did not. Truly, how was I to know I might already be with child? It was my first knowing of a man, and only once."

"Dare I ask who knew you before your husband?" My voice took on a coldness I did not want, but my words were out and I could not swallow them.

"Mother, please." Her teary eyes pleaded.

"Obed?"

"Yes, I love him. I should not have married Azel.

Remember when Obed came to get me two weeks before the wedding? We let our passions get the upper hand when we were together. When I had been studying with Serena, Obed and I occasionally stole away to take walks, and we became close friends. Part of the reason I wanted to keep my studies to be a healer was so I could see him again. I was foolish."

"You are young, and you have many years ahead of you. Does Obed know you might carry his child?"

"He may suspect it, but I have not told him. I do not know if he is aware of how many moons a woman carries a baby until birth. I do hope Azel will not keep a count of the time."

"Marian, Marian, Azel has children, so he will know. When will you tell him? Does he know you are here?"

"Azel was away when I left. A trusted house servant is to give him the message I went to see Serena. He knows I am with child, so he will understand I went to the healer for help. Two house servants brought me to Serena in the carriage and then returned home."

"Did you ever approach Azel about learning healing arts?"

"No, I did not ask again. The day never seemed right. He was busy and had no time to talk, and he would need to be away tending to business. I became ill in the mornings and took to my bed for a time. A kitchen servant who brought me broth told me she thought I was with child. There was always something."

"I love you, and Azel adores you completely and treats you with kindness. You will love the infant right away. When the baby is born, I believe Azel will accept it as his."

Serena came in and laid her hand on Marian's abdomen. "You are experiencing tightness in your middle. There will be more squeezing as the baby moves out. Any pain?"

"Not much right now. I feel as if I have eaten something causing distress in my belly."

Serena continued to hold her hand on Marian and count quietly. "When I feel your middle, it is hard like a melon rind." Her stoic expression did not change. "The birthing stool is here for you as you are ready to give birth." Serena stayed with her.

I remained by Marian's side, giving her whatever comfort a mother can at such a time. The night wore on and I grew tired. Thinking it would be a while longer, I went outside to breathe. The dark sky, illuminated with twinkling stars, seemed like a promise all would be well. As I was coming in the doorway, I heard her panting, crying, and screaming, and I knew the birth was happening. All became quiet for a little while. Delightfully, I heard my grandchild cry, and it sent a thrill into my being and mind I cannot describe. Serena called, "Tabitha, come to see your grandson."

Teary-eyed with joy, I hurried to see him. Serena tied and cut the baby's umbilical cord. She lifted the boy for me to see. I took him, wet and warm into my arms. He was small and perfect.

"Mother, I feel incredibly tired, but I am whole again. I no longer wish to die. I have to live for my son. Put him on my breast, please."

I put the tiny newborn onto her breast for a few minutes and then took him to clean his body with salted water and wrap him with a swaddling cloth. He made little sucking noises and put his thumb up to his pink lips. With a perfect round bald head, he had a few strands of fine dark hair. His eyes were closed, and he had no eyelashes.

"I will send a runner to tell Azel." Serena was cleaning up as she spoke. "The infant is small, but perfectly formed. He came earlier than his time, but he will be all right." She summoned a servant to come help her.

"Will Marian be well?" I asked. My daughter's pale face shone with perspiration, and her hair was a tangle of matted brown spirals on the white cloth.

"She needs rest and nourishment. Encourage her to drink some broth," Serena said. She smiled and tugged playfully at Marian's big toe. "You did well."

"I am well, but I think I shall not want to go through this again for some time." She cupped the baby's little face and lightly kissed it all over, like a butterfly. "Now the pain has gone and left me with an adorable son."

"You will be fine." I went to the hearth to ladle some broth from the open kettle into a cup for her. I felt the happiest I had been in a while. Our seed would go on in this beautiful little one. Jacob would have been proud to see a grandson.

As she sipped the broth, Marian kept looking at her baby with an expression of love and wonder. I was surprised when she looked at me and said, "Did anyone tell Obed?"

"I do not believe so." My happy moment shattered as I realized my daughter had come to Azel after she had intimately known Obed. Her life could be complicated by this transgression. There was nothing I could do but stand by and support her.

"It does not matter. Azel will take good care of us. Our son was born early." Marian looked happy and relaxed. "He has thin fingernails like fly wings, only pink." She laughed.

In the morning, I heard a knock on the outer door. Serena was busy, and no servant responded, so I answered. I was surprised to see Obed, as I thought he would be at work with Phillip. He should have known not to come. I wanted to send him on his way until I saw his young face tight with worry.

"How is Marian?" He had an anxious look in his eyes, and his arms dangled by his sides like limp rags.

"She is doing well, and so is my grandson."

Obed's tanned face softened in relief. "Thank you, um, I suppose I will be off to the metal shop then." He turned and left.

"Who was talking with you?" Marian asked.

"It was Obed, and I told him you were both well." I

tucked in her covers and removed the half-empty broth cup.

"Thank you. I am perspiring under the cover, and I think I have soaked the rag under me."

I helped Marian wash and put a clean cloth under her, comforting her by smoothing her hair. She drifted to sleep with a peaceful look on her face.

A servant had been dispatched to tell Azel and Samuel. Azel sent word with a messenger he was overjoyed to hear he had a son and his wife was well. He would be arriving before the eighth day to circumcise his son. Marian was happy to hear the news her husband was on his way.

I stayed with Marian and encouraged her to soften her nipples with olive oil and gave her advice on nursing her baby. All was well. Serena was glad to have me take care of Marian, as she was busy with other patients.

Azel was beaming with pride when he arrived. "God has blessed me at my great age to once again have a son. My young wife is such a gift to me. Praise to the Lord of all. I am here for the *Brit Milah*." He performed the circumcision and said all the prayers. They named the boy *Joktan*. It was a joyful, wonderful day, and I was pleased to be with them. His servants brought a horse-drawn cart where Marian and the baby were bedded on luxurious, soft cushions and rugs for their trip home.

"Will you be going to Joppa?" Marian's young eyes glistened and pleaded with me not to go.

"Would you like for me to stay with you for a time?"

I knew her response without her saying a word.

"Please come. You are welcome in our home, and you may live with us as long as you wish," Azel said.

"I would be pleased to go with you to help and become acquainted with my grandson, but I will stay no more than a short time."

"Mother, thank you. I want you to be with me," Marian said. "I am unable to be close to my husband due to my uncleanness."

I went along in the comfortable carriage to their beautiful home. A room was prepared for me. Joktan slept during the ride, waking to nurse and go back to sleep. His light brown eyes were crossed at first, but in two days began to focus and sought Marian's face. To me, he was tiny and beautiful, and I could not be happier.

Days passed as we settled into a life built around Joktan. He started having a bit of stomach ailment, and the evenings were filled with his wailing. A serving woman, Elia, brought a wet nurse so Marian could sleep, but she waved them away and walked the floor, patting Joktan to soothe him. When she tired, I laid him on his stomach on my lap and gently rubbed his little back. I experienced peace as he quieted with my touch.

Their kitchen servants prepared wonderful meals. I marveled at the pottery and crockery from Azel's trading afar. There were flat-rimmed baking dishes they placed in the oven in which they combined eggs, herbs, spices, and vegetables in a way I had never tasted. It was delicious.

Azel came in one day and said, "Joktan, you have a good voice. Some day we will have you singing psalms." He laughed, and took the child, cradling him in his arms and speaking in his deep soothing way. "You try too hard, my son. You must be patient with us as we get to know you."

Samuel and Lottie came to visit. "What a beautiful child." Her eyes were wide with questions, but she wisely kept them to herself. It was early to tell, but the boy seemed to have many of Marian's features, especially the eyes and brows. The few strands of dark hair he had at birth had fallen off, and a golden-brown bit of fuzz began to emerge. He reminded me of Marian when she was a baby.

Lottie and I went for a walk. She had kept her curiosity until then. "Was this not soon after the wedding?"

"He was born early, small as you can see, but well-formed and healthy."

"Was Obed there?"

"Yes, managing Phillip's metal shop, and he inquired as to Marian and the baby's well-being, but nothing more."

"Will Marian stay with Azel?"

"There is no question. Azel is delighted to have another son after all these years. He adores Marian and the boy. Why are you making something out of nothing?"

"I am not trying to make something out of nothing. You remember when the two youngsters ran off together to Serena's."

"Yes, I know all too well. My daughter has confessed to having romantic feelings for Obed, but she said he would not want to be tied down to a wife and family."

We were quiet for a moment, and I asked, "How are things with you and Samuel?"

"I have been well, but I feel lonely without Marian or you nearby. Will you ever return to your hut?" Her face was sad, eyes downcast.

"Marian and Azel invited me to stay for as long as I would like, and I will remain while Marian is getting accustomed to caring for her baby. I do not want to go to my hut and be alone. There are many bad memories there."

"Only memories. Samuel wanted to believe Uzziah died, but there was no blood along the trail, and his body disappeared."

"I hope the Lord took care of him in some way." I did not tell her of my seeing Uzziah in Joppa, either ghost or real.

"You are kind to think of his well-being." Lottie shook her head and smiled at me. "You have good work to do in Joppa?"

"I sew for people and help a group of widows in particular who have become friends."

When we went inside, Marian was walking and

patting Joktan's back as he was drifting off to sleep in her arms. I said, "Nothing looks more peaceful than a baby sleeping in his mother's arms. He is growing, and becoming keenly aware of his surroundings every day."

"I know. He is becoming livelier by the day, and I am proud to be his mother. His mouth formed a little smile at me. Marian kissed the top of his head.

"May I hold him?" Lottie looked at them with longing, her arms outstretched.

"Let him sleep when I give him to you. Does he not look like me?"

"Yes, and it pleases me." Lottie sat down and held the baby.

Samuel rushed in, a look of concern on his face. "Lottie, we must go soon."

"Joktan is peaceful on my lap, and I have been sitting with him but a minute." Lottie shook her head sadly. "What can be so urgent, Samuel? Please give me a little time with him."

He did not sit down. "We may come another day and visit. I am truly sorry, but I would like to leave now."

I knew not to question Samuel, or any man, when they decided it was time to go. We gave our last hugs and kisses to them, and they left. Joktan had awakened but took no time to be snuggled up to Marian again.

I was delighted to see her being the mother she was meant to be. "Do you think you will ever study with Serena?"

"I may want to, but I cannot with Joktan in my

arms." She sighed contentedly. "Serena told me about another young woman, a shepherdess she taught years ago. She said I reminded her of the girl, Hannah, who may have attended the woman who bore Jesus." Marian cuddled her son as she talked and walked, holding him until he was asleep.

"I have not heard of the midwife, but I have listened to stories about Jesus from the widows in Joppa and visitors at Simon's house. It could be true, but Jesus died by crucifixion when he and his followers stirred up trouble in Jerusalem. Some have said he did not stay in the tomb but rose from the dead and walks among us," I said. "Difficult to believe."

"Rose from the dead?" Marian did not look at me for a time. "Mother, what happened to Uncle Uzziah? I know he was bad and he drank to excess, but Samuel said he disappeared after a bad quarrel the two of you had."

My hands became clammy. My daughter recalled a night I wanted to forget, but I thought I must tell her the truth. "Yes, we argued outside, and he was violent with me. He hurt me, and I defended myself by hitting him with a staff. He was knocked out and had no breath. Samuel heard me screaming and came. We both thought Uzziah was dead, but when Samuel returned later with help to bring the body to the house, your uncle had disappeared."

"So, he could be alive somewhere?"

"I think not."

"If he died, does it mean you . . .?" Marian's words trailed off.

I nodded. "Yes."

She looked kindly toward me, and said, "I am sorry, Mother."

I had mixed feelings as I left the next day to return to Joppa, accompanied by one of Azel's servants who led me on a donkey as he walked beside me. The weather had cooled, and our walk was not unpleasant. We stopped to rest at night. I did not sleep, and was alert to any noise or people on the trail, as I worried Uzziah could be alive and looking for me.

Twenty-Eight

U zziah had been fishing with Daniel for some weeks, and they sometimes had hours when they conversed with nods or signals each understood. One day, fish were not going into the net, and Daniel stretched his legs in the damp boat. He drew out a flask of wine and took several long draughts on it before he handed it to Uzziah. The warm sun moved in and out of the veil of clouds. Seabirds called overhead. Uzziah felt peaceful as they basked, lulled by Daniel's quiet acceptance of the situation.

"Did you have only one brother?" Daniel asked.

Uzziah was startled by the question and sat up to answer. "Yes. His name was Jacob."

Daniel tipped the flask to his lips. "Caleb and I were the only sons, and we learned to fish from our father. He died when I was eleven, Caleb fifteen. We took the boat out together and fished for a living, cared for our mother and sister. Caleb was bossy and we argued often, came to fists sometimes. He was bigger and won. He was interested in finding ways to make more money. When I was fifteen, we worked for tradesmen who set out in a larger sailing vessel and traveled to ports across the Great Sea. We were the ones to unload cargo."

"Did you make a lot of money like he thought you would? Was the cargo loading hard?"

"Yes, we did but worked harder. We were unloading heavy packs of iron, and I was to guide the suspended bundle onto the dock. The rope broke and the huge bunch of iron fell onto me, and pinned my arm, crushed it. I was in dire pain. A healer severed my arm so it would not rot and cause me to die. I was hurt physically, and also in my spirits. It took a long time to get over it." Daniel tilted the flask and lay back in the boat. "I suppose I am fortunate to be alive."

Uzziah did not know what to say and fell silent as his companion's eyes were shut. Daniel was through talking but had left much unsaid about his brother.

In the evening after they had supped with Mary, he asked Uzziah if he would like to go into the town. They entered a noisy place with a beamed ceiling filled with men at tables refreshing themselves with strong drink and rounds of bread after a long day at sea. Daniel ordered cups of beer for them at the counter which they took to a corner bench amid the echoing hum of conversation. Uzziah preferred wine over beer, but did not want to offend Daniel by refusing the drink. The place smelled of old wine, strange spices, sweat, and fish. They drank slowly and relaxed for a while.

"I am sorry about your arm, the pain, and loss," Uzziah said.

"It was Caleb's fault I am maimed. But I can fish, and I found a good wife." He sounded proud, yet gazed into his drink as he rasped out the words.

"Did Caleb have a wife?"

"Yes, and two daughters."

"You did not have to take care of his wife?"

"No." They went to refill their drinks and returned to the bench. There was a long pause. Uzziah watched men talking and laughing, not unlike the days when he had gone away to drink and forget his troubles.

"I was not married like you, and I was legally bound to take Jacob's widow as my wife."

"She died then?"

"No. She hated being my wife and tried to kill me the last time I saw her."

"Why did she hate you?'

"I was not like my brother."

"You fled the dangerous little woman?" He laughed and took another swallow. "Sometimes my wife sees Caleb's wife in town. Last time Mary saw Delia she was wearing a new tunic."

"Caleb left her with money?"

"No, she lives with a group of widows. Mary says there is a new widow in town who sews for them."

"Jacob's wife sewed all the time and liked it better than anything."

"Ever wish you could see Jacob one more time?" He drained his cup and sighed.

"Yes, sometimes. Do you miss Caleb so much you want to talk with him?"

The air in the room seemed to be thick and the voices in the air became louder as if someone were urging them on.

Daniel's eyes were glazed and he breathed deeply. He began to rise from his stool then settled down. "Yes, I wish I knew if he was dead."

"What do you mean?" Uzziah sat forward, blinking.

"His boat came to shore without him or his crewman."

"He may be alive somewhere." Both had finished their drinks. Men were leaving as most all would be out early fishing again.

They rose from their seats as if by a signal and walked toward home. The sky was bright enough with a half-moon and stars in their courses in the black sky.

"One of the women we saw a few days ago at market looked like Meydl Tabitha."

"The young one was pretty."

"Jacob had a beautiful wife."

"Too bad you could not make peace with one such as her." He clapped him on his shoulder.

"I cannot make peace with her." His fists clenched. "First, I must settle a score since she left me to die."

Twenty-Nine

I was in Joppa, having stopped at Simon and Elena's home on my way. James and John were there proclaiming the message of Jesus and the gift of the Holy Spirit he had given them. It was a lot to take in when they asked me to spread the good news of a loving and forgiving God who had sacrificed his son. I was confused. They wanted us to go to the sea where they would baptize Simon, Elena, and me. I watched them baptize Simon by immersing him in the sea. John said, "I baptize you. Be blessed by the Father of Jesus."

I waded into the cool water, hopeful yet apprehensive, as I had not been in water like this. I felt foolish and fearful, turned away, and waded toward the shore. I did not want the baptism as I did not understand what it would do for me. I doubted a man rose from the dead. After they came out of the sea, I asked John. "Is the Father of Jesus the God I have always believed in?"

"Yes, he is and more. He has given us his son to die and rise again from the dead to prepare a place for all people when we die. He promised to return."

"I wish to see him for myself." My skirt was soggy and cold. It seemed improper to me to be there with men.

"I think Jesus will return soon," he said.

"I look forward to seeing your Jesus, but I do not want the baptism." The cool, gritty sand clung to my feet.

"We will see you again." Elena had watched the baptism but not participated. She came to me, and we laughed at our damp embrace. Simon and Elena went to their home. I walked to Joppa and put John's message out of my mind.

"I am happy to see you. I missed you." Sarah opened the door, and we kissed cheeks.

"Were there any night door knocks while I was away?"

"No, thankfully, nothing to frighten me." Sarah gave me a hug and I returned it.

News I was in town spread among my friends, and they gathered in our home. We supped together as they welcomed me back. Before I left, I had started a project of seeking widows who needed clothing but were ashamed to ask for help. When any of them went to visit, they offered to help in any way. I became busier and had a number of tunics, cloaks, and other clothing to sew. I hoped Marian would send word to me how everyone was doing.

Much as I had tried, I could not get the thought out of my mind. What had become of Uzziah the night when I was sure I had slain him? John had told me, "If you have done wrong, you are forgiven by Jesus."

I wanted to trust I was forgiven as I had asked, but the guilt did not leave me. The way I hoped to pay for the grievous sin of killing a man was to work diligently helping people. Sewing was a pleasure, so I could not in good conscience count it as hard work. I did my stitching, especially when vexed by breaking threads, as if I did it to atone for my sin.

One day as I sat sewing in the sunlight streaming from the upper window, my stitches went well, and my thread did not break. I heard a knock on the door. Assuming it was one of the widows, I did not rise but called, "Come in."

The door opened, but no one entered. "Is this the place I will find Tabitha, eh?"

I dropped my sewing to the floor and rushed to Zeke. My heart fluttered with joy as I had missed him and wondered what had happened to my benefactor. "Zeke, oh, Zeke!" We embraced and his beard brushed my face as we kissed cheeks. He smelled of fresh sea air and clean sweat.

"Simon said I would find you here, eh. He told me what you have done with the materials I left in the sack."

"I cannot thank you enough for the fabrics as I

have made many garments for needy widows and their families. Will you please come in and sup?"

"Yes. My donkeys are tied outside. I have brought sandals from a man with whom I trade and would like for you to have them, a gift, eh." He stepped outside and came in with two pair of sandals. "And I have another thing I found when you are ready for it."

"Thank you. I cannot thank you enough. May I give one pair to someone who needs them? My friend Sarah goes barefoot."

"They are both for you to do as you would like, eh." He paused and had such a pleasant demeanor as he gazed at me. "I remember walking with you many miles. Your old sandals must be worn away, eh."

"The sandals I wore then are gone. You are kind to remember. Please sit here on the mat and I will bring wine and bread." I slipped a pair of sandals on my feet and walked around so he could see they fit nicely.

Zeke smiled and sat down, groaning a bit as he let his body settle on a cushion on the floor. He looked the same as when I had last seen him, perhaps whiter hair, but the same rotund body. "It feels good to see you doing well. I worried about you, how you would get on all alone, but I see you are with others now, eh."

I sat beside him on a cushion as I poured wine into cups and offered him a loaf of bread and soft cheese. I wondered if he forgot he said he had something else for me and could not imagine what it could be. "When will you bring out the very strong thread you have found?"

"Oh, it would be good if I had found such a thing, but this gold ring might have belonged to your deceased husband as years ago your father-in-law wore one like it." He drew it out of the pack at his waist.

I could not believe my eyes. It was the same as the signet ring Uzziah wore. Jacob had a similar ring he had seldom worn as he was afraid of losing it when he worked. I became unsettled, and the room seemed to be spinning. I lifted my wine cup but set it down as my hand trembled. "How?"

"I did not mean to upset you, my dear. A man who was trading rings, buckles, earrings and such gave it to me for a small carpet. I liked it, as it was well made, but when I studied it further, I knew I had to bring it to you, eh."

"It is not Jacob's ring. I gave his ring to Marian and she has it to give to Joktan. I do not know how this man came to have it, but it is like Uzziah's ring. He was wearing it the night . . ." Fear clutched my chest, and I had difficulty breathing.

Zeke reached over to pat my hand and comfort me. "I am sorry I brought the ring. It has made you afraid of something or brought you some bad memory."

"It has made me fearful Uzziah could be alive and may have sold his father's ring for food or money on which to live."

"I think it more likely a robber found his body, stole the ring and anything else he had on his person, and disposed of him, eh. It was traded for other goods, so do not worry. All will be well with you as you do good works, eh." He paused, sipped wine and tore off a piece of bread to eat.

"I am feeling useful and have good company. My work is to make clothing for any who are in need. A young woman named Sarah lives with me. She is due to have a baby and needed a place to stay. You may meet her when she returns from market."

"Very well. The bread is the best I have had. You baked it, eh?"

"Yes, I did. Are you traveling afar to buy and sell wares?"

"Yes, and it is lonely." He grew quiet and looked steadily into his wine cup as if there were something inside he wished to see.

"What adventures have you had the past years?"

"A few, as it happens. I am slower, with weariness in my feet and painful stirrings in my back, eh. When I was near to your lands, I heard your neighbors had a visit from the tax collectors. They kept their property, eh, but sent a large portion of their grain as tax payment."

He sipped his wine. "Your daughter's servant had a baby boy with her, and gave me water at the well."

"My grandson Joktan! I am glad you saw him." I paused, sipped wine, and nothing was said. "Zeke, I remember fondly how we traveled together, and I am grateful."

"It was good. When you were with me, I felt young. You were like a daughter, eh."

"A daughter." The affection I had for him was like the brother I had not had. He was a wonderful friend.

"Even one I could care for more than myself. More than anyone, eh." He looked at me with smiling eyes.

"I have the same feelings for you, dear Zeke. You gave me hope and opened for me a life I could not have dreamed of by myself once I had lost everything else." Tears welled in my eyes.

"Eh?" His kind eyes looked into mine and then closed as one rolling up a scroll after reading. "Did you ever find unbreakable thread?"

"No, I have sewn many stitches and broken many threads in my life and never have found it." We laughed together.

"Whether it is thread or not, someday I trust you will find something unbreakable and unbroken, eh. You have a good life in Joppa helping widows with your sewing."

"Yes, it is satisfying, and all I need." We ate and drank in silence, each of us not wanting to break the quiet bond of friendship we shared. After a while, he rose stiffly from the cushion. I stood.

"I will be off, dear Tabitha, and I wish you well, eh. I hope to see you sometime. Remember me to your God, so he may be good to you and to me, eh." His voice grew soft as one who is out of breath. His beard brushed my face as he kissed my wet cheeks, and he turned and closed the door.

Zeke was gone. I feared I would not see him again.

It was as if some part of my life had come to an end, as when Jacob had died, or I gave my last coins a long time ago. Was there still a future for me? Only the Lord of Heaven knew.

In the days after, I sometimes went without food, as I was not hungry. Sarah gave birth to a daughter, Eunice. I had another to care for, but I longed to see my own daughter and grandson and prayed to the Lord to keep them in his care.

When Eunice was fussy because of colic, I relieved Sarah by taking the baby onto my lap. One night when I was walking the floor with the crying infant, I began to feel dizzy and had to sit. Sarah was lying on her bed resting, but not asleep. "Are you not well?"

"My head felt faint. I will be all right." I put the baby next to her, and she fell asleep. I went to my bed. It was the first of many times I felt ill. Day after day, I weakened. Esther suggested I see a healer and brought one to the house. The woman did not reside there but was nomadic. She was in Joppa as she and her husband had been traveling with some disciples of Jesus.

When she came into the house, she went first to little Eunice who was on the floor playing. "Sweet child, you are blessed to be with such fine women. I had no children of my own but raised others." She was dressed plainly and had a light scarf wrapped around her hair. She turned to me. "Are you the one who seeks a healer?"

"Yes, I am Tabitha."

She appeared radiant and ageless when she came

near. She took my hand, looked at my eyes, and touched my cheek. "I cannot say what your illness may be, but here are some herbs to take. Put them in a broth for the best taste and add vegetables." She turned to Sarah. "Cook them well in your round pot." Strands of brown hair crept out of her head covering.

"Which vegetables?" Sarah asked.

"Any you have will do. I believe you need more nourishment, as your bones have little flesh and your eyes have lost their luster. If you have a lamb bone, boil it, and add the good broth to your vegetable soup with the herbs. It will give you strength." She put the herbs on the table for Sarah.

"How soon will I feel well?"

"In a day or two, you should see improvement. I am not staying in Joppa, so you will be on your own. You must eat, and bed rest is important. If you do not feel improved, seek a local healer. Believe in Jesus and trust him to heal you."

"Thank you," I said.

"Trust in the Lord for all your needs. He knows more than anything we can understand. Talk with him, and he will show you the way you must go." We kissed cheeks as she left. I forgot to ask her name, but there was an aura about her I would not easily forget.

I recovered some in two days and began sewing tunics for the children of the widows. They grew out of their clothing fast. Women came and brought food for us. Esther found paid sewing jobs for me, and I worked long hours to earn enough to buy materials to sew for the needy. While I tried to eat well, my strength never returned.

"Tabitha!" Sarah called to me one morning when I did not rise. "What can I do for you?" Her eyes squinted with concern as she knelt beside my sleeping mat.

I could not move my legs. I stayed abed and could do nothing but sleep. I fell into a deep slumber in which I heard Sarah's faint voice. "Tabitha, are you thirsty or hungry?"

"Tabitha, wake up. You cannot continue this way." Esther sounded concerned.

I was aware of other women as someone spoke urgently, alarmed. "I am going to let her family know, for it appears she is dying."

Thirty

heir voices took on the sound of whispered panic, and I thought they were not near.

"I think she has no life in her. Send some men to Lydda and tell Peter we need him," Bithiah said.

"Peter is a disciple of Jesus, but can he heal as Jesus did?" Sarah sounded doubtful. "You must let Simon and Elena know she has died, and they can send messengers to her people," Sarah said.

I heard people weeping. Their voices trailed off. I wanted to tell them I only slept, but my limbs were like logs, and I could not move or speak.

I heard a baby cooing, or perhaps a dove. The echo of people came and went like the ebb and flow of the waves on the shore in Joppa. "I fear she has died." I could not tell who spoke. I heard weeping.

"Meydl, come." My father's words echoed. I wondered how and why he was where I could hear him as he was dead long ago.

"I am waiting," Jacob assured me. Then my surroundings were white like I was inside a cloud for a time, and abruptly Father's and Jacob's voices were gone. It was the darkest night. The absence of sound was alarming. Then, a yellow and black striped demon spun me around, buzzed and laughed, and tormented me with thorns and hot coals. The swirling was like a whirlwind that did not stop. I was terribly cold and helpless, and I wanted to scream for someone to come to my aid, but I was mute. Light once more, a steep cliff face stretched before me, and I had to climb up. A dark sea beckoned below. It was treacherous and there were few protrusions of rock or branches to hold onto. I grasped a tree stump, but it gave way. I slipped, falling into an abyss. It was an endless seeming tumble and took my breath away. I frantically grabbed onto a jutting rock and held it. My fingers burned red until I could hold on no longer. I pleaded, "Lord, save me."

I heard a voice, "Tabitha, you have done as I asked and busied your hands to sew for the needy." I was in a room filled with cloth and thread, so I thought it meant I should continue to do my stitching for others. The thread was torn into short strands. Why was the thread broken? I wanted to tie them, but they were out of my reach. How could I keep making clothing for the needy?

"You have done one thing well, but have neglected the more important part." My inner being longed to hear what I had done wrong. Would this be the day I was held accountable for Uzziah's death?

"You have doubts," a voice intoned. What did I lack? My mind pondered hard, yet I could not think of anything. The silence overwhelmed me. I was mute and could not ask what I should do.

The voice broke the quiet. "Jesus, God's son, died and rose from the dead. You do not believe it." The buzzing demon whirled into my vision again and the noise was deafening. The fabrics and thread had disappeared, and I heard no more. Naked, frozen inside and out, I needed a heavy cloak like Jacob wore. It appeared too far away for me to reach.

How could I answer the charge against me? Was I lost? Was my life gone? I could not scream, but pled in my mind, "How can I believe? Please help my unbelief."

"Therein is the whole thread, unbreakable and unbroken," said the Voice.

I drifted like a feather in the wind, whirling upward, but I was not dizzy. Nothing mattered anymore. I was free to move to and fro as if dancing to ethereal music. I was dew on the grass. I was vapor in the air. I was part of everything. My peaceful feeling was like nothing I had ever experienced before. I do not know how long I was in such a beautiful place. A warm gentle breeze wafted in my face.

"Tabitha, wake up." I heard a man's insistent command, but I could not recognize his voice and did not want to leave my peaceful habitation. I was not sick or worried or thirsty, and I wanted to stay. It was only the man's voice and no other sounds. Warm life-giving breath blew gently upon me as his words became more urgent. "Tabitha, in the name of Jesus, arise!"

I opened my eyes, not sure if I was on my bed or some distant place I had drifted. The man's tanned face came into view. He had a strong jaw and concerned dark brown eyes, and a curly beard. "Tabitha, you still have work to do here."

I wanted to stay in my wonderful dreamy state, yet thought I must speak if I could. I whispered, "Who are you?"

"Peter. I was summoned from Lydda because you died. Your friends and family were grieved and wanted me to bring you back to life. The women all tore their clothes. They sobbed and showed me the beautiful garments you made for them, then prayed and urged me to raise you from death. Restoring your life was not done by my own strength or ability, but by the power of the Almighty Lord's risen son."

"Where am I?" My eyes closed, but my body began to feel solid again. I no longer floated about and became aware of my arms and legs beneath coverlets. Slowly, I sat up and took a deep breath. It was as if I had risen from turmoil and now had new life.

In a strong, urgent voice, he called to the women downstairs. "Sarah, Esther, come and give Tabitha something to eat."

"She is alive!" I heard them exclaim.

"You were dead, and he raised you," Esther said, as

she came to me and grasped my hand.

"I was asleep and dreaming of fearful, daunting things and beautiful, strange places. I cannot tell you about it now."

"Tabitha, oh, Tabitha, Peter brought you back to life. I have some broth for you." Sarah, aglow and smiling, held a brown clay cup in her hands.

"Our God had compassion and restored her," Peter said.

I was overwhelmed by what they told me. My hands looked softer than when I had clung to the rock. I had no scratches or scrapes, and there was no sign of the soiled cloth and broken thread. I accepted the cup of soup. "Thank you."

Sarah brought Eunice to me, and she opened her arms to be on my lap. I put down my broth and held the baby. She gurgled contentedly as I patted her. And I smiled. "I wish I could see my grandson Joktan and my daughter."

"We sent word to your family and a horse-drawn carriage is on its way," Sarah said.

Thirty-One

Uzziah tossed and turned in bed thinking about Meydl Tabitha he had lusted after before she tried to kill him. What if she was the woman he had seen in Joppa? He hoped she was so he could confront her and punish her for trying to kill him and leaving him for dead. Why had she been an obstinate and cold wife? Had she not had everything a man could provide? Her home was comfortable, and the crops profitable before she lost it all to fire and taxation. His eyes blurred. Perhaps it was the night of strong drink which he had not had for some time, but he fell asleep and dreamed of the wife he wanted. He awakened early to fish.

The next day as they were on the dock sorting fish to sell, he heard a familiar young voice. "Is it really you, Uzziah? I thought I would not see you again."

"Silas, what brings you to Joppa? You did not leave your parents, did you?"

"No," he said as he came nearer.

"You have grown taller since I saw you. I cannot believe it has been so long." Uzziah met the boy, and they clasped forearms despite the fishy grime on his arms. "Are your mother and father here, and are they well?"

"My parents are alright, but we are grieved as grandfather died. We brought him home to bury and are all here to trade and go on our way again. I asked my father if I could go to the docks to watch the boats, and he said I could as long as I did not take an oar, row, and not return."

"I am sad your grandfather died." He kept staring at the boy who was almost a man. "I think you did not expect to see me here."

"You are far from your hut."

"I could not stay there, so I walked all the way to Joppa, where I have become a fisherman."

"We taught you how to throw a net." Silas puffed out his chest.

"I have helped him learn much more," said Daniel.

"Silas, this is Daniel, with whom I have been fishing. He is much more experienced, and I have gleaned great knowledge from him."

"If you are staying awhile, you could come with us early tomorrow," Daniel said.

"I would like to."

"No running away from your parents." Uzziah clapped him on the shoulder. "Tell them you have a chance to see the vastness of the Great Sea."

He saw that Silas lingered as they moved on to sell fish. Daniel handed Silas a string of six fish to take with him. "If I do not see you again, have a good life, Silas," Uzziah said.

Early the next day Uzziah looked at the people nearby. He saw the usual men getting their boats ready to go out. When they were ready to take up their oars and leave, they saw Silas at a distance with Wills. They waved to each other, and Uzziah breathed a sigh of relief. The boy he felt brotherly love for had chosen the better part, to obey his father.

After a day of fishing, Daniel and Uzziah were on their way home. There were people standing outside the place Uzziah had seen the woman who looked like his wife. They all appeared sad, and a couple of women with torn tunics were weeping. "What happened here?" Daniel asked Delia.

"It is Tabitha. She has died. Mary will tell you about it when you get home." Her voice quavered as she turned away.

When they arrived at home, Mary greeted them. "How was the catch?"

"It was good," Daniel said.

"There is something sad going on down the road. Delia told me a woman who made the garments for all the widows has died. Tabitha has not lived here long, but they all loved her for her compassion and kindness," Mary said.

Uzziah was stunned into silence. He thought the woman might have been Meydl Tabitha, who could have changed her name to only Tabitha. Jacob said she always hated her first name. Uzziah sat at the table with them but had little desire for food.

"Come on, eat," Daniel said, as he broke some bread to take another bite. "We have to make an early start tomorrow to beat the storm."

"The food is delicious, but I cannot eat much." Uzziah took a few bites of fish stew and sopped bread into the bowl.

"You think the woman who died could have been your wife," Daniel said.

Uzziah nodded. "Thank you for the meal. I cleaned my hands in your bucket before I ate, but I want to go to the well to give myself a good wash."

"We should go down the street and find out for sure who died." Daniel cuffed him on the shoulder. They both stood and went to see what had happened.

When they approached the house, there were more people outside talking among themselves. "What has happened here?" Uzziah asked a man who was near.

"Tabitha has been raised from the dead by Peter. It is a miracle and proof of the resurrection of Jesus," the man said.

Uzziah shook his head. "May I go and see for myself?"

"We cannot let a stranger in now. Who are you?"

"I am brother to her deceased husband. She is my

lawful wife."

"Let him in," Delia said when she saw he was with Daniel. "She will say whether or not."

Uzziah fought the urge to leave. He did not know what he would say to her, or if she would speak with him. He was ushered into the room by two women. She was seated on cushions. He stopped breathing when he saw it was her. Lamplight highlighted her radiant face and soft tresses. She was more beautiful than he remembered. He wanted to turn away swiftly, but her eyes caught his.

A look of disbelief and shock was on her face, but she shook her head as if she had not seen him. She turned to the baby on her lap.

He wondered whose child it was, and came a little closer. "Meydl Tabitha, it is Uzziah."

Thirty-Two

I know who you are, and I am no longer afraid of you. I was dead, and I am alive again." Uzziah stood in front of me, looking at me with the same arrogance I had seen so many times. "I do not know by what means you live today, but you are forgiven for your ill-treatment of me. I am grateful you are alive. Please forgive me for hitting you so hard you fell and hit your head on a stone." I reached into a small bag attached to my belt. "My friend traded a nice rug for this signet ring. I do not know how you lost it, but I believe it is yours."

Uzziah stood gaping at the sight of his ring. His voice was shaking, and he could not look at me. "Where did you find it?"

"It was given to me by Zeke the Rug Man. I am glad to restore it to you as a sign of forgiveness."

He did not reach out his hand to receive the ring. "I am surprised and grateful, yet . . ." His voice trailed off as if he had lost his thoughts. "I have become a fisherman as my mother's kinsmen were, and I have changed. If you want to be my wife, if you will have me as husband. I am living with Daniel and Mary down the road from here."

"It is your ring." He did not reach for the ring greedily as I had expected. He looked perplexed, uncharacteristically quiet. I continued to hold my open palm out to him. "Please put it on your finger where it belongs."

His composure returned, and he sneered like the Uzziah I remembered as he snatched the ring from my hand. He put it on his finger and clenched his fist at his side. "You made a name for yourself here and look too proud to ever be a fisherman's wife."

I hesitated, then said, "Go in peace. Now let me be." I meant it and hoped Uzziah did not still hope to avenge the horrible blow I brought him down with years ago. He had not divorced me so he was still my husband. I did not see Uzziah slip out of the room. I did not know how long I would live, nor did I know if there was another purpose for me in life. I knew with certainty I had been raised by the power of our Lord through Peter and I was at peace.

Somewhere among the crowd of people who had come to the house to see the miracle of my resurrection, I heard a familiar voice, "No better woman lives than Tabitha, eh?"

"We agree!" Their voices trilled like birds singing.

"I am alive," I said and quietly answered the voice I no longer doubted who was my Lord and Savior. "I believe Jesus was raised from the dead for everyone."

"You found an unbroken thread at last," Zeke said, as he shuffled toward me and put a hand on my shoulder. We kissed cheeks as happy tears rolled down my face.

"Jesus is unbreakable and unbroken."

Glossary

Baal – A farm god of the Phoenicians and Canaanites

Bar mitzvah – When a Jewish boy reaches age 13, the ceremony denoting adulthood is celebrated.

Brit Milah – Circumcision, a ceremony on the eighth day after birth, where a baby boy's foreskin is removed.

Chuppah - The canopy for a wedding ceremony.

Erusin – Formal engagement ceremony

The Festival of Booths – Also sukkot, an agricultural holiday.

Girdle – A belt worn around the waist of a garment.

Great Sea - Mediterranean Sea

Homer – Six and one-fourth bushels

Hora – A festive dance

Ketubah – Prior to marriage, the legal obligations of the husband were read and signed by two neighbors as witnesses. The wife's obligations were understood and not read.

L'Hayim – A salute to life and health.

Meydl - (Pronounced - MAY-dil) – Yiddish, meaning girl.

Mezuza – Doorpost. Bible verses on a parchment are inserted in a small case on Jewish doorposts.

Mites – Small coins worth less than a penny.

Pan – A Greek god in charge of nature, forests, and animals.

Psalms - Religious poems or songs.

Purim – A Jewish holiday celebrating Queen Esther's saving her fellow Jews from genocide.

Son – (Pronounced zoon) – son.

Tabitha – Gazelle. Greek language, Dorcas

Talitha – Little girl

Tishri – Jewish calendar month like September.

Wadi Charith – Brook Charith

Zealots - The Zealots were originally a political movement in first century Second Temple Judaism which sought to incite the people to rebel against the Roman Empire and expel it from the Holy Land.

About The Author

E. Ruth Harder

Elsie Ruth Dornbusch grew up on a farm in Uvalde County Texas. She married Charles Harder (deceased, 2003) in 1957. She was a Technical Information Specialist at Lawrence Livermore National Laboratory until retirement. Achieved a Masters in Library Science from San Jose State University in San Jose, California. She says, "Critique groups and workshops of the California Writers Club, Tri-Valley Branch help keep me motivated as I pursue my passion for writing."

Advances in Library Administration and Organization, Vol. 13, 1995, published her work, "Library Automation's Effect on the Interior Design of California Public Libraries." She has written scripture–based puppet scripts performed for children at Sunday morning worship at Holy Cross Lutheran Church in Livermore. Her poem "Widow's Window," is published in the *2014 California Writers Club, Tri-Valley Branch anthology, Encore*. "A Light in Every Corner" is in *2014 Word Movers, An Anthology of Creative Writings by Seniors. Hannah Weaver of Life, 2015*, Russian Hill Press.

"Daily prayer and Bible studies and my Holy Cross Lutheran Church family and those at Faith Lutheran in Kamiah, Idaho, both keep me focused on what is most important in my life, the eternal blessings of our Lord and Savior, Jesus Christ."